For Everything There Is A Season

A Season

Surviving After A Spouse's Death

Dr. Clarise Hairston Ottley

Gonna Be Okay Publishing

ISBN: paperback 979-8-9897510-0-6

ebook: 979-8-9897510-1-3

Cover design: nOahKEaton

Published by Gonna Be Okay Publishing

For

Mrs. Anna Rose Anderson

Thank you for your comfort,
empathy, kindness, and wisdom

Contents

Prologue

I never actually saw her.

Though we only talked by phone, those two hours resulted in me loving her.

Mrs. Anna Rose Anderson was not the first person I met who had lost a spouse. There were many. Yet she was the one who made the biggest impact in my journey of widowhood. She spoke with such ease and gratitude. Instead of counting her loss, she treasured her gain. She felt thankful for the years she shared with her husband and for her amazing God who she found to be completely trustworthy.

Before our conversation ended, I knew I wanted to be like her. She modeled the ability to move forward with grace, peace, and appreciation for the gift her husband had been.

To linger, long for, and pine after that which they had together was not her way.

"If you can think of things about your husband that were good," she counseled, "his death will not hold you in bondage."

At 95 years old, Mrs. Anna Rose recalled the events of her husband's death as though they were yesterday. A widow for 61 years, she found contentment and solace in God's Word. That is a lot of winters, springs, summers, and autumns without the man of her dreams.

When the season that made her a widow came knocking at her door, she could open the door and embrace it, or try to fight this very real and very unwelcome visitor. She gathered her emotions, mental stability, and physical stamina and changed with that season. Though she felt like crumbling, she recognized the task before her.

No longer Mrs. Anderson, wife of Mr. Anderson, Anna Rose was reborn with a fresh identity and a new way of thinking about this new life God had invited her to live.

Mrs. Anna Rose died a year after sharing her story with me. She will not have an opportunity to read this book, but her testimony will live on in the hearts of the women who will read about her seasons of life.

At her eulogy, I knew the title of this book should be *For Everything There Is A Season.* According to her pastor, Ecclesiastes 3: 1-5 was one of her favorite scriptures. "For everything, there is a season. A time for every matter under the heaven: a time to be born and a time to die; a time to plant, and a time to pluck up what is planted; a time to kill and a time to heal; a time to break down, and a time to build up; a time to weep, and a time to laugh; a time to mourn, and a time to dance; a time to cast away stones, and a time to gather stones together; a time to embrace."

Mrs. Anna Rose taught me how to dance in the cold, drenching rains that appear in the winter seasons of life.

Chapter One

Shattered

As I walked down the aisle, there was no celebration and no beautiful gown. I didn't choose bridesmaids or the colors of their dresses.

When I married him, my whole world changed. Now my world had changed again. This time, I walked down the aisle alone. My friends who had been my bridesmaids wore black.

The words "I do," signifying that we had chosen each other, would never again be uttered from my lips to his ears. On this day of sorrow, loss, and pain, family and friends had gathered with me to say goodbye.

He had traveled all over the world, but he always came home. When he left for Barbados for a few days of vacation with our son, I thought that he would return.

Earlier, we took a trip to Italy with one of his long-time friends. Despite what the medical reports had said, Al could not walk 50 feet without becoming breathless. Out of embarrassment, he told us to go ahead and he would catch up.

"Al," his friend said, "I've never seen you this large. You promised me you were going to lose weight. You're killing yourself."

"I know," Al responded. "I'm going to get help. I can't do this by myself."

Years of trying multiple things and using many weight loss programs only yielded temporary results. He would lose fifty pounds and gain back that much and more. At 150 pounds overweight, the doctor said he qualified for Bariatric Surgery. Al knew this was the only way he could get his weight under control.

The life-saving procedure was scheduled for November. He passed a battery of tests including intensive cardiopulmonary tests, pulmonary tests, psychiatric tests, physical therapy, and weight loss programs to assure he was healthy enough to undergo the Bariatric Surgery.

Although the test results were negative for risk factors, Al had been having some health challenges that none of the team of doctors could identify.

I'm a nurse. I was taught to listen and look at the patient instead of machines. The test results should mimic what is seen. Yet, for months, his respiratory status did not mimic the cardiopulmonary test results. Each month, Al kept an appointment with the cardiologist and pulmonologist. What I saw was completely contrary to what he was being told.

But how do I refute the test?

As Al prepared for the trip to Barbados, I advised him not to go before seeking medical attention in the States. Days before he was due to leave, he had passed out.

"I promise," he said, "I'll have a physical when I return."

According to our son, the time with his father had been uneventful, although I asked him to keep a watchful eye. Hearing about the episode, my son tried to convince his dad not to come to Barbados.

"You know your mother," Al had said. "She is always overly concerned. I'll be fine."

You Are Not Alone

According to the U.S. Census Bureau, as of 2019, there were almost 11.4 million widows. For many, becoming a widow can be both devastating and heartbreaking. Widowhood happens to approximately one million women each year.

The median age for women, when they become a widow, is 59.4 years old. Half of women over the age of 65 will outlive their husbands by 15 years leaving emotions of loneliness, despair, and the trauma of financial burden.

If only they could be made aware of the emotions and everything we continue to go through when a husband dies. But if such a book exists that warns on the statistics of widowhood, I doubt I would have read it either.

Aside from the pain and loss of a spouse, which is devastating by itself, the other concern is the negative impact on finances. The Social Security Administration reports the rate of poverty among elderly widows, which consequently is any woman 40 to 65, is three to four times higher than what their husband would experience if their wife died.

If you are an elderly woman and are not impoverished, when your husband dies you may face financial adjustments that will take your breath. There may be a decrease in income, loss of health insurance, or the need to sell your house and relocate. Too often the after-effects are a combination of these. Each has the ability to destroy you physically, emotionally, and financially.

In early widowhood, a widow's grief can parallel what has been called a *brain freeze*, where their recall becomes weak. They develop short attention spans and their decision-making capability is difficult if not impossible. They may temporarily forget their social security number, or where they placed important documents. Leaving something in an unfamiliar place results in searching for an item like car keys for hours and sometimes days. Many unsettling moments are spent wondering what day, month, and year it is.

This part of grief is so intense that no words can describe the mourning that goes on and on without relief. As my pastor said, "Mourning is not the destination, it is the journey."

Chapter Two

Wherever He Is

Whenever Al traveled, he always called when he landed at his destination. Occasionally, when he stayed over a day or two to get extra miles from the airline carriers, he let me know his plans. This time I did not get a call.

His flight from Barbados was scheduled to land at 10:30 p.m. Since I did not hear anything from him about giving up his seat on the plane in exchange for a voucher or money, I assumed he was on schedule to return. I anticipated he would call from his car around 11:00 p.m. to say he was driving home from the airport.

The airport was 90 minutes away and I estimated he would arrive at midnight. I stayed awake in anticipation of seeing his face light up when he saw the new comforter, shams, and curtains.

Before he left, he said, "Aren't you tired of that comforter?"

Unlike me, Al was keenly perceptive of his surroundings while I could not see something even as I walked over it. Until his question, I had not noticed the spread that had been on the bed for two years.

Having been up since 5:00 a.m. I laid down on top of the new comforter to rest my eyes. I dozed until awakened by the familiar sounds of Al coming through the door and disarming the alarm. A glance at the clock showed midnight.

Good, he's home, right on time.

I thought I heard the usual noises of him rooting in the kitchen for a snack like he usually did when he came home. He frequently turned on the TV to unwind after travel. Soon, I knew he would be upstairs, and this time I would see the excitement of the new decor on his face,

My alarm woke me at 4:00 a.m. Looking to his side of the bed, Al was not there.

Odd that he didn't come upstairs. Maybe he fell asleep in the recliner.

Yet, when I went downstairs, he was not there. The TV was off, and there was no luggage.

I know I heard him. Where was he?

A sinking feeling came over me. Often, he sat in the car with the motor running as he listened to a radio mystery or the news. Of course, he left the garage door open until the program concluded. But, what if this time he closed the garage door?

Breathless, I flung open the door that led to the garage. His car was not parked inside.

Rushing upstairs to check my phone, my heart pounded at the thought that there could be a message with news I did not want to hear. Had my husband called and I didn't hear my phone ring? Had he been in an accident?

But there were no messages. No text.

My call to Al's cell phone went to his voicemail. *His plane must have been delayed. He couldn't call because he was still flying.*

But a glance at the time told me that was unrealistic.

"Oh, God," I said aloud. "Did his plane crash?"

I turned on the news, and there was no mention of a crash.

A call to the airline confirmed that he had checked in on Saturday for his flight which departed at 1:00 p.m. on Sunday.

My voice shook as I asked the next question. "Can you confirm that he was on board that plane?"

"I'm sorry," she said, "I cannot confirm whether he boarded."

Desperate for clues, I tried another direction. "Did the flight depart on time?"

Through the phone came the quick sound of keyboard clicks. "The flight left on schedule," came the reply, "and also landed on time."

Panic flooded my veins. Had he been in an accident on the back roads between the airport and our house? At that hour of the night, would anybody come to his aid? What if he had passed out again? Or fell asleep while driving?

I called the highway patrol in Maryland, Virginia, and West Virginia. No, they assured me, there had been no report of an accident on the route that he would have taken.

But what route was that? Which airport had he scheduled to fly into? Knowing he was with our son, I hadn't paid a lot of attention to the travel details.

Next, I called the hospitals in our area. The emergency rooms from Baltimore, Washington DC, and Fairfax said the same thing, "We cannot give you that information."

"I just need to know if my husband arrived at your hospital."

"Sorry ma'am," each repeated their practiced speech, "that is–"

"A HIPAA violation." I finished their sentences. "Please, I'm a nurse, and I know hospitals cannot give out that information because of patient confidentiality. But he didn't come home." I stifled a sob. "I don't know what else to do."

A glance at the clock showed it was 6:00 a.m. Where was Al?

My call to our son went straight to voicemail. "Your dad did not come home last night," I said into the recording. I called our son many times over the next hour, hoping that he would answer. Each time my heart raced faster at each voicemail message. He often placed his phone on the do not disturb setting. Had Al told our son of a change in plans? While there was no reason for this to be the case, I was thinking of any possible scenarios to calm my growing panic.

Having exhausted everything I could think to do, I knelt and prayed for Al's safety. "God in heaven, please let him be safe wherever he is."

Because I couldn't think of any other words, this was my sole request. I desperately prayed these same words over and over again.

Chapter Three

Gone

Brushing tears from my face, I either had to get ready for work or call and explain that I would not come in for my shift.

What good would it do to call out? Wandering through the house and wringing my hands while I waited for news was not helpful. Yet, what good would it do to go? Could I concentrate?

I thought about the people relying on me to prepare payroll. Staff depended on me for guidance, and I was training someone today. I dressed and drove to work.

At the office, the clinical coordinator met with me to learn how to do payroll. As my thoughts replayed the moments last night when I felt Al had returned home and settled in, it was clear that had only been my imagination or a dream. It was not a reality.

"My husband did not come home last night," I told the clinical coordinator. "I don't know where he is."

She asked the questions I had already asked myself. "Is there anyone else who would have an idea where to look for him?"

The only option I had not explored was the fraternity brother who owned the condominium where Al had stayed.

"Al did not come home last night," I said when his fraternity brother answered my call.

This friend immediately made a three-way call to the manager of the condominium.

"I went by Sunday afternoon to see if Al was gone," the manager reported. "I tried to enter, but the deadbolt was locked from the inside."

My voice quaked. "Do you think he was there?"

"I saw his car outside," she affirmed. "I assumed he decided to stay longer."

"Perhaps Al is ill." I grasped for hope. "Maybe he fainted again."

His fraternity brother spoke to the manager. "Have maintenance remove the deadbolt."

While the three-way call remained connected, the maintenance guy arrived and opened the door.

"Do you see him?" I waited for the manager's reply.

"He's in bed," she said.

Didn't Al hear the maintenance man working on the door? I heard the manager call his name. I held my breath, longing for the familiar sound of his voice in response. The silence felt heavy.

"Please," I pulled on my nurse's training, "see if he is breathing."

"I don't see signs of him breathing."

"Is he wearing his CPAP mask?"

"Yes."

Taking a deep breath, I asked for what I needed next. "Will you touch his face?"

After a pause she answered. "His face is ice cold."

My heart broke. *Oh, God. Oh, God. Oh, God.*

"Put a mirror under his nose," his fraternity brother instructed. "See if the mirror fogs."

I heard the manager rummaging through her purse. After a long silence, she spoke again. "No."

"Begin CPR," the owner said.

"Wait," I broke in. "Tell me what his body looks like." I wished I could be there to put my fingers on my beloved's cheek. "How does his skin feel?"

"His arms are cold." She was quiet for a moment. "His tongue is blue."

I swallowed back the lump that suddenly blocked my throat. "There is no need to perform CPR."

"Clarise, she is there, she can try–"

"No." I squeezed my eyes closed against the tears. "He's dead."

Chapter Four

We're Going To Be Okay

D ead.

My legs buckled and the clinical coordinator who was in the room, guided me to a chair.

All I could visualize was my dear husband lying there. No one had been with him as he transitioned. I had not been there to hold him.

This can't be.

From far away, I heard his fraternity brother ask the office manager to phone the police and coroner. I wanted to scream. To protest that this could not be true.

But I didn't. I wanted to cry, but the tears that had threatened earlier would not come. Instead, my body and mind felt paralyzed. Numb.

"Clarise." The office manager, whom I had met several times, called my name. "Clarise, I'm so sorry. Is there someone I can call for you in Barbados?"

I did not know the phone numbers of any of his relatives in Barbados. "No."

Our three-way call had been on speaker so my clinical coordinator heard the conversation. "Clarise," she hugged me. "I'm so very sorry. Who can I call?"

I met her eyes but my mouth refused to say any words. She patted my shoulder and notified staff and coworkers who rushed to my aid. Through tears, several asked how they could help.

"I need to call my sons."

My first call was to my son I tried to reach earlier that morning.

He answered right away. "Mom, what's going on? I have five calls from you."

"Your dad never came home," I said. "He died in his sleep in Barbados."

"Dad was fine when he took me to the airport." He was silent for so long that I asked if he was still there.

At last he asked, "Do you know what happened?"

"The coroner is on his way. Maybe we will get some answers."

I told my other son that his father died.

"I'm sorry, Mom." His voice was tender. "How did grandaddy pass?"

"Not granddaddy." Slowly, carefully, I repeated the words that his father was gone.

"No." Then louder, "I need to see it to believe it."

My third son wanted to know when, how, and where. I gave the scant details I knew.

"Mom," his voice was soft and comforting. "You're going to be okay."

That's what Al said when I was miserably sick with each pregnancy. "Honey, you're going to be okay." And I was. Somehow, I had to be okay now.

My other son had been so intricately involved in his father's life that I felt concerned about what his reaction would be to this devastating news. If he took this hard, I would not be able to bear his sorrow in addition to my own. "Please," I asked my oldest son, "tell your brother for me."

The youngest called within minutes. "Are you okay?"

I assured him that I would be. "What about you?"

"Yes, Mom," he answered. "We will all be okay."

A staff member called the airport to make reservations for me, along with one of my sons and daughter-in-law. We would leave later that day.

"I'll pay you back."

"Don't you worry about that right now," she said. "I love you."

A staff member drove me home in my car while a coworker followed in her car. Numb with shock and sadness, the thought of Al being dead was like a scene from a movie. The leading cast member, I was a woman who just lost her husband. He was irreplaceable. That scene played over and over in my head during the drive home.

Friends and relatives quickly gathered at my house, offering condolences and help. I gave my phone to a friend and she made calls to relatives and other friends who lived nearby. Soon, my address swarmed with people who loved me and my husband.

When I saw my cousin who lived in Winchester, the pent-up tears erupted and I began to sob. Although she had not lost her husband, I could feel in her embrace that she understood.

Al's only sibling lived on the West Coast. "Diane," I said to my sister-in-law when she answered the phone, "Al's dead."

"What?"

"Something happened while he was asleep in Barbados."

She let out a deep wail that echoes in my mind today. "Not my brother."

The brokenness in her voice tore at my heart and I handed the phone to my close friend to continue the dialogue. Al and Diane were very close. Their father had been gone for more than 50 years, and they lost their mother seven years ago. All the family they had were each other.

At 88 years old, Uncle Tommy was Al's oldest living uncle. Al often visited him in New York. The family in New York called my husband Freddy. Like Diane, Uncle Tommy cried out, "No, not Freddy."

Completing the few phone calls I had to personally make, I felt physically and emotionally too weak to call anyone else. I could not bear to hear the pain and shock of anyone else.

My pastor and his wife arrived. Al mentored our pastor during his new hire and the two of them had created a strong bond of love and appreciation over a short period. Seeing the grief in his eyes as he embraced me nearly brought me to my knees. I wept, and he and his wife comforted me.

Someone reminded me that our flight was leaving from Baltimore at 1:00 p.m. I needed to pack quickly.

"What do I need?" For the life of me I couldn't remember what to pack. "What do I take?"

People moved fast. Food was ordered for those who had come to help and share condolences. Others tossed things into a suitcase and gathered documents I would need on the island. Besides clothes for one day, maybe two days, I tried to remember what Al packed on his frequent trips to Barbados. What would I need for this quick turn-around? A driver's license, passport, my medicine, and documents to identify Al's body.

Suddenly the reality of what was happening pressed in on me. "Oh God, I cannot do this. Please, Jesus, help me." I said this desperate prayer over and over.

From the files, I retrieved my passport. I gasped to see the expiration date was April 30, 2017. Today was May 8, 2017. *How can I get my passport renewed in time to catch my flight?*

Someone read my face and called the Passport Office. The person at the passport office told them I had 30 days from the printed expiration date before the passport officially expired. God made a way through the wilderness. "See, I am doing a new thing! Now it springs up; do you not perceive it? I am making a way in the wilderness and streams in the wasteland," Isaiah 43:19 NIV.

That's when my mind and heart calmed. Aware of God's presence, I stopped striving. God reminded me He was in control and worthy of my trust. Anticipating the upcoming flight and my phobia of flying, the Lord affirmed, "He who keeps Israel, neither slumbers nor sleeps," (NIV). He would keep me and my family safe.

My son and his wife arrived as I was being helped into the car. I don't remember who drove us to the airport. The best we could do was a layover for the night and catch a flight to Barbados the next morning.

Who is going to lock up my house? Who is going to make those dreaded calls to my family, to Al's family? I had all the numbers in my phone but could not make any calls in the air.

I later learned that everyone who had Facebook shared the tragic loss. A friend found our address book at the house and took care of many of the important notifications. "But God who is able to do exceedingly abundantly beyond what I could ask or think," Ephesians 3:20 NIV.

The flight to Ft. Lauderdale was less than two hours. "Lord, this can't be happening," I prayed over and over. "My husband can't be dead."

My son interrupted my thoughts. "Mom, are you okay?"

I said "Yes, are you okay?"

"Mom, we're going to be okay." His words jolted my spirit. They were the same words my other son had said when he heard the news.

I have four wonderful sons, all gifts from God. He used Al and me to bring them into this world. As their only living parent now, I had to pull myself together for my sons. Yes, I lost a husband, but they lost a father. I had known Al one year before we were married. I was his wife for 38 years. They had known him as their father all of their lives.

Once we landed at Ft. Lauderdale, I checked with the gentleman at the airline counter in regard to my passport. He assured me that I would not have any trouble based on the date of expiration. I had to trust God that what he said was true.

My son, who had been vacationing with his father days before, met us at the airport. Al's closest fraternity brother flew in to join us on our trip to Barbados. We embraced each other like no other time, signifying we both understood the loss and, out of respect for each other's feelings, we chose to be strong and not cry.

We rode together to the hotel, a short distance from the airport, to spend the night. Our next flight was early the next morning for the second leg of the trip. My other son did not have his passport so he could not go with us. When his dad dropped him off at the airport, he had gone home, unpacked his things, including his passport, then flew to Ft. Lauderdale to meet some friends. He was able to meet us and make sure we were going to be okay.

I was far from okay, but I had to pretend to be fine for the sake of my sons. Would I ever truly be okay again? I was about to do something that I had said I would never want to do, and that was to identify the body of someone I loved. For most of the night I prayed, "Lord gives me strength to handle tomorrow."

Chapter Five

Discrepancy

Tuesday morning, I met my sons and family friend in the hotel lobby to catch the first shuttle. At the airport, I went immediately to the airline counter to show them my passport. Just like the man told me the night before, there was a 30-day grace period. Hearing the same message three times was an assurance for me.

Dreading what I would have to face, the four-hour flight to Barbados felt like 18-hours. "God, make it go away," I begged. "Wake me from this bad dream."

"Remember Psalm 23, Clarise," a friend had advised, "you must walk through the valley of the shadow of death. Some things you have to walk through to get to where God has purposed for you to be."

Once we landed in Barbados, Al's fraternity brother arranged for a taxi to take us directly to the morgue. The morgue closed at 2:00 p.m. and we were still sitting in the car at 1:00 p.m.,while the driver tried to start the engine.

"God, I'm trusting You to go through this now, not tomorrow. Please help the car to start." In minutes, we were on our way.

We arrived at the morgue five minutes before closing and the doors were locked.

"God," I prayed, "we need your help again."

My son and Al's friend banged on the doors and the windows. Finally, a man opened the door.

I told him Al's name and showed proof of my identity and my marriage certificate. He led us to a room and told us to wait.

When he returned, he asked, "Are you ready?"

My heart yearned to say no. Identifying him would mean his life with me was really over. Anxiety rose inside and I could hardly breathe.

My son broke the silence. "Mom, I'm going with you."

I didn't want him to see his dad's body pulled out of a drawer. "I'm going to be okay."

He repeated the words he said over the phone when I broke the news to him. "The only way I'm going to believe Dad is dead is if I see him for myself."

Together, he and I, and his wife followed the man to where Al's body had been since they found him on Monday.

"The coroner estimated his death to be Sunday," the man cautioned. "Now it is Tuesday."

How could I prepare myself? Would he appear disfigured? Would he show signs of distress which meant he died in agony all alone?

The man pulled open the drawer and removed the cloth covering the face of the body. I summoned every ounce of strength to maintain my composure. I wanted to scream, "God, please no! This can't be happening."

I longed to call his name. Like I had done for so many years, to say, "It's time to wake up, Honey." Instead, I touched his face and knew this was my new reality. My husband was dead.

The guy at the morgue gave me an envelope. Inside were Al's wedding bands I had placed on his finger on our wedding day in 1979, and in 2004 when we renewed our vows 25 years later. Also, inside this bag were his gold chain with a cross he never took off even when he had a surgical procedure; his money clip; his wallet with his ID; and his passport. I did not need any of these items to tell me the body that I looked at was my husband.

We stood in that hot and humid morgue, examining his face, hoping for some movement. Maybe he was in a coma. If he would only wiggle some part of his body, we could take him to the hospital.

My son and I examined his body and spoke softly as if talking louder would disturb the other people in drawers.

"Dad got his wish," my son said. "Countless times he said he prayed that he would die in his sleep."

"Because the thought of dying any other way was not the way he wanted to go." I finished the memory. "God granted his request."

The morgue keeper's voice interrupted my thoughts. "He'll need to go back in the cooler very soon."

My son met my eyes. We knew we had to say good-bye. With a last glance at Al, we turned away. I didn't want to see my husband pushed back inside that drawer.

Neither of us cried, I think for each other's sake.

Returning to the outer room where Al's friend waited, my legs felt as if they were not able to hold me up. My son took my arm and supported me.

"He's gone," I said to Al's friend. From the devastated look on his face, I knew he had been holding on to hope. Like us, he hoped the person in the morgue drawer was not dead, or was not Al.

Following his examination tomorrow, the medical examiner would declare the cause of death. I wanted to stay in Barbados to hear the findings. What caused his death? Did he have some condition not detected by his doctors? How could they have missed this? What were the signs? I am a nurse. Shouldn't I have noticed something? I was the one who spent my life with him.

My son interrupted my thoughts. "It's time to go, Mom."

But I wanted answers. I wanted to blame someone for what had happened to my husband.

The next day, a few hours before we had to leave for the airport, the medical examiner phoned. Miraculously, as if God heard my unspoken need, he asked if he could come by.

"The cause of your husband's death," he said gently, "was his heart. It just stopped beating while he was asleep." He explained that the underlying cause was cardiomyopathy. Al did not have a heart attack. He did not suffer. His heart simply gave out.

Knowing that he did not suffer gave me peace.

The death certificate listed May 7 as Al's final day, but the autopsy report revealed that he died on May 6. The discrepancy in dates would prove to be a problem.

On the flight home, I recalled the last time I spoke with Al. We talked on Friday before he was scheduled to return on Sunday. The conversation was ever so brief. While it was not our practice to talk every day, we would text frequently. I knew we would talk Sunday, if not sooner because he always reached out either before his flight took off or as soon as he landed.

If I had known that Friday was our last conversation, I would have talked longer. I would have told him that I loved him, not just the usual comment before saying goodbye or good night, but that I truly loved him.

Both of us loved one another, but I could not say that we had always been *in love* with each other. Our love was enough to sustain our marriage for so many years. Two weeks before Al died, we experienced a sweet confirmation of the kind of love we shared. Like a cleansing of the soul, we were happy to start a new chapter together, with God's promise, "See, I am doing a new thing...." Isaiah 43:19.

Al and I looked forward to the years ahead as we grew old together. We anticipated the joy we would experience as grandparents. Our two-year-old and three-year-old granddaughters called him Poppie. Sadly, their memories of him would be faint now that he was gone while they were yet so young.

Chapter Six

Memorial

While I knew that redoing a death certificate or birth certificate in Barbados takes a long time when compared to the US. I was not prepared mentally, emotionally, or physically for the extended delay.

We could not move forward with a funeral because we did not know when his body would arrive in the United States. My family and I waited for days which turned into weeks.

A retiree from the US State Department, my brother wrote a letter to the Consular requesting his assistance in handling clearances and local government coordination needed for the return of my husband's body. In addition, he made several calls over the course of the weeks asking, almost pleading on my behalf. The Consular said that this type of change on a death certificate was out of his control and at the mercy of the court of the registry.

After three weeks, we longed for closure. My family needed to go back to work and try to make sense of what normal life would be without their father. We decided to plan a memorial service for a

Monday without his body. Having a plan, even if his body was not back, was something I needed.

The memorial ceremony was as intimate as I could make it, with 20 poster-size photos of Al from infancy to his current age of 70. My family and I planned for the wake to occur a couple of hours prior to the ceremony.

People streamed in by the hundreds to pay their respects. I stood for two hours greeting friends who lived near and far. Many, I knew, made a sacrifice to come and their presence touched my heart. Tears welled as people I had not seen in years arrived at the memorial service.

My daddy, who was 83 years old, drove six hours to be with me and his presence meant the world. My mother, in a nursing home and suffering from dementia, wasn't able to attend. I missed my mother whose loving arms would have brought comfort to my broken heart.

After the service on Monday, word came that his body would arrive Wednesday. The funeral home I had contacted to receive his body confirmed that all went according to schedule.

The funeral director telephoned. "Do you want to bring his clothes and verify this is Al?"

I thought about this for a moment. "You are our good friend, you know us well. Can you verify that it is my husband?"

"Yes, Clarise," he assured solemnly. "It's him." To sidestep the added emotional agony for me of choosing clothes for Al and bringing them to the funeral home, he suggested we have a closed casket.

"Thank you," I replied.

On Friday, we held a small graveside ceremony attended by Al's immediate family and a few close friends. Al's longtime friend, doctor, and elder in our church, took charge. The gathering was brief and full of expressions of the grief that he felt having lost a brother in Christ.

At my husband's graveside, I recalled a conversation Al and I had about our wishes when one of us died before the other.

"I want to be cremated," Al had told me.

"I don't know if I can honor that request," I said. "It's so opposite of what I would want."

"But you must agree to cremate me," he insisted.

I had smirked. "And if I don't, you will not care because you will be with Jesus, in the happiest place we all look forward to, with no concerns."

Now, I realized all we went through in the previous weeks could have been avoided if I had complied with his wishes.

"Clarise," the friend conducting the ceremony interrupted my thoughts. "Would you like to say something?"

I had not prepared words to say, but words flowed. I cannot remember what I said yet I know they were words from God because as I spoke, I could see the impact on every person present. I followed my words with what I believe to be true, expressed eloquently in the song, *How Great Is Our God*. Perhaps that song was for me because I felt a release of Al into the arms of God.

Chapter Seven

Counsel

Several months after Al died, I noticed a waning of my friends. After a year, only a few married friends and hardly any single friends came to my home or invited me to do things.

There was a time I felt abundant with friends, single and married. We shared plenty of activities from pajama parties to movies. Al's job was in Minnesota, a distance too far to commute. He stayed in an apartment during the week and came home weekends. Some weekends I traveled to his apartment. During the six years we lived with that schedule, I cultivated close bonds with a group of female friends.

I do not know if they knew, but for the first year after Al's death was when I needed them most. But they were not there. Though no longer married, I was still me.

Were these seasonal friends? Relationships that were in my life for only a period of time? Perhaps they felt awkward and did not know what to say. The reality was I did not need them to say anything, just be with me. Listen, let me cry, and offer the comfort of their presence.

Most said, "If you need anything, call me."

But as a new widow, how did I know what I needed? I felt empty. Numb. Lonely. Suffocating. All of these at the same time.

I read that loneliness is having plenty of people to do something with but no one to do anything with. When there were plenty of friends and we had fun, the room roared with laughter. But when Al died, the room became silent as I found myself alone time and again.

Reality was my friends felt helpless, and what I needed was my husband. Without my friends, I finally realized my loneliness was deeper than my husband's death. I had never been alone before. As an only child, I was always with my cousins. As an adult, I always had friends. And as a married woman, I was always with my children and family.

I was acquainted with Christian counselors. My husband and I sought counseling a couple of times when we hit rough spots in our marriage. Each time, we saw what we perceived to be a mountain was merely a molehill.

After Al's death, I went to the same counselor we both had seen because I felt comfortable sharing my heart. The counselor assured me that God said throughout the Bible that He would care for me. Although I hated the title, I found comfort in what God had to say about widows.

The counselor noted I was no longer a married woman. Single again, I had much more to offer God as He had even better things in store for me.

As winter approached, I could not make the long trips to the counselor's office, so he recommended someone closer to me. This counselor said God had given to Al the gift of me.

In a way, God said to Al, "I gave you the opportunity for 38 years to take care of her. Now I will take over from here."

"Expect God to do exponentially more than you could ask or think," the counselor said. "He is going to meet all your spiritual, physical, emotional, and financial needs. You are His daughter, His treasure."

Believing God put both counselors in my life to speak empowerment to my heart, I took God's words and applied them. God had even greater plans for me ahead. In 2 Kings 4:1-7, God made a promise to provide for that widow. God sustained me as I walked through that dark valley, and all along the way. "My cup overflows. Surely your goodness and love will follow me all the days of my life," Psalm 23:1-6.

While I was confident God would supply my needs, I did not know what I needed other than to not wake up every morning realizing my husband was gone and would never come back.

How could I feel better and move forward from this horrible, life draining grief and sorrow? The pain was insurmountable, crushing away my breath so I felt I was going to collapse under the weight.

If I could find a step-by-step book for how-to live after losing my husband, perhaps such a resource would ease the pain. But there is no such book that can remove the agony of any widow's broken heart and grief.

This book will not do that either.

Jesus said He came to mend broken hearts. Through my sons, their wives, grandchildren, friends, colleagues, associates, father, aunts, uncles, first cousins, and the neighbor next door, Jesus mended my heartache.

These precious people sympathized with me. Some phoned, some never said a word while their sorrow showed in their eyes. Many prayed for me. One friend checked on me weekly. The considerateness of such gestures were healing when combined with time.

"There is a time for everything, and a season for every activity under the heavens: a time to be born and a time to die, a time to plant and a time to uproot, a time to kill and a time to heal, a time to tear down and a time to build, a time to weep and a time to laugh, a time to weep, and a time to dance, a time to scatter stones and a time to gather them, a time to embrace and a time to refrain from embracing, a time to search and a time to give up, a time to keep and a time to throw away, a time to tear and a time to mend, a time, a time to be silent, and a time to speak," Ecclesiastes 3:1-7.

Nothing is included in the Word of God by happenstance. God said, "Blessed are those that mourn, for they shall be comforted," Matthew 5:4. I know His Word is true, and I know He can't lie, so I sought God and His Word.

"You turned my wailing into dancing, you removed my sackcloth and clothed me with joy, that my heart may sing your praises and not be silent, LORD my God, I will praise you forever," Psalm 30:11-12. I've learned to draw nearer to Him for comfort in what seemed like a never-ending grief cycle. I tried to be strong for our four sons, daughters, grandchildren, and for those around me whose lives were impacted by his death.

I learned God doesn't want me to hurt, and He doesn't want me to spend my days crying. He wants me to live and help others to do the same. That is why I am still here. Paul said the things that happened to him were intentional for the furtherance of the gospel. Even this, Lord.

Chapter Eight

Shift

The death of my spouse, followed by the death of my mother eight months later proved devastating. The sorrow I felt and the weight on my mental, physical, and spiritual shoulders were overwhelming.

During the loss of my husband, I also dealt with the loss of friends. Was I alone?

No. God was present just like He had always been and as He had promised. According to Psalm 139:13-16, before I was born, He knew this situation would happen.

Now, I can thank God for allowing some friends to scatter. The solitude brought me closer to Him as I had time to think, cry, reflect, and come to grips with my past, present, and what lay ahead.

I had to trust Him to heal my broken heart and remind me that He gives purpose to my life. God fulfills His purpose in me and grows my faith. When I lack faith, He provides that as well. He is able to do beyond and above what I could ask, think, or imagine.

God met my need by providing lifetime friends, some of which were cousins that I've known for more than 60 years. My first cousin may not live close, but she checks on me often and will come if I really need her. Through thick and thin, highs and lows, she is a source of love and support throughout the years. "A friend loves at all times," describes Proverbs 17:17.

I learned not to cry over friends who I thought were forever relationships but were not. However, it is wisdom to hold close to true friends. These companions of the heart are exactly what is needed when a spouse dies.

Because I was the first person in my social circle to lose my husband, I felt this was a part of God's plan for them. I will be there for them.

Moving Forward

To move forward meant daily pressing through my pain. I showed up for worship team practice. On Sunday mornings, I scraped together every ounce of energy to go to church and sing.

"Lord," I prayed, "to your glory. Therefore strengthen me to make it. Strengthen me to give You praise."

Sunday night I arrived to teach the women's Bible study. I gathered my emotions because these women needed me to share what God had given to me for each of them.

One of my best friends had lost her son many years before Al died. Another friend's marriage had ended in divorce. There were close friends living outside of God's will for their lives. Several others were fighting for their lives as they battled cancer.

God let me know emphatically and empirically that fulfilling my purpose was not about me. He would use me to bring healing to these women's pain. Month after month, I shifted my focus to serve others despite what I was going through.

Making life less about me and more for others felt good. It was as if God designed my life to be a magnet that drew people with hurts to me. They came from work, friends, family, and church. Did they ever wonder how I was doing? Thought about what I needed? Each time I focused on myself, God reminded me that this was not about me. My time would come later.

"Clarise, you have served others for your whole life. Now it's time for you to reap what you have sown," a good friend said. "Instead of teaching, place yourself in a position where you can be taught God's Word from others. Allow people to pour into your life at a time when you will need them most instead of you pouring into their lives."

I really needed her words when Al died. She said to accept encouragement instead of always giving it. Be still and hear God speak through other people about His plans for my life instead of me speaking about what God has in store for others.

Every chance that appeared, I listened to sermons in church and online. I found an app that provided moments of meditation that I continue to listen to today. People prayed for me instead of me praying for them. Friends from my women's group assisted whenever I had a need.

My music minister often asked, "How can I pray for you?"

I felt I could say exactly what I needed and he would pray.

Soon, I was able to move forward like never before. Like pouring fresh oil, God restored my strength to serve when I didn't want to admit I was depleted.

God was doing a new thing in me as I allowed myself to rest in His arms. He fed me and carried me when I felt too weak to go on. God's Word says, "God is able to do exceedingly abundantly beyond what I could ask or think, according to the power that works in me," Ephesians 3:20.

God is the power every woman needs when she finds herself a widow. His power continues to work within to aid me in moving forward. "It is God who arms me with strength and keeps my way secure," 2 Samuel 22:33.

The enemy of our souls whispers lies in our ears. Thoughts that bring defeat, downheartedness, and hopelessness are not from the Lord. Quickly trade those lies for God's promises that bring hope and lift our face to Him.

Recalling when I was in a low, desperate place, God spoke the word *shift* to my heart. Every time I encounter challenges, trials, and negative feelings I remember that I can shift every aspect of my life. I move my thoughts toward God, His command, direction, and lead.

"If you are bent over by what you are going through, the devil can ride," my grandmother often said. "Stand straight, and he will have to fall off."

I choose to stand and I choose to shift my eyes, my thoughts, and my focus on God. He turned my mourning into dancing in this winter season of my life.

Chapter Nine

A Prayer For Such a Time As This

My hope is this resource is a helpful companion for those who will experience what I, and the ten women who share their testimony in these pages, went through. Before you read further, let me pray for you, for me, and for us.

I pray, Father, for the widows who read this book. I pray for those women who have no idea that they will be a widow in the future. I ask that each finds the same strength I found, and the women who shared their testimonies found during their many moments of grief. Our desire is that God be glorified.

Father, I ask You strengthen those who read this book by the power of your Holy Spirit, so they can bring glory to You. It is a part of your marvelous purpose and plan for them.

Help them not to fear or be dismayed for You are with them. You are their God. "I will strengthen you, I will help you; I will uphold you with my righteous right hand," Isaiah 41:10.

I pray You send someone along who will be Your arms to hold and cry with them. Please provide what they need from people who care.

Father, affirm any woman who is despondent or has anger toward You for allowing their husbands to die. I know that anger towards a God who loves them sounds very harsh yet You know our deepest feelings. Through Your love and tender care, help each one trust and be restored. You see them right where they are. You are with them even now.

God, you promised, and therefore it will come to pass, that in this season of loss, you would pour out peace. Starting today may Your peace be what these widows come to know.

Father, thank You for being present in their lives, their rear guard and front guard, a present help in time of trouble. The day their husbands died was not a surprise to You. In Your wisdom and perfect will, You left each woman here.

Nothing takes you by surprise. You knew way before you sent them from heaven to their mother's womb that they would experience the loss of their husbands. Yet, Oh Lord, You give all they need for this experience. You've quietly prepared their hearts and thoughts to endure such a loss.

"But you, Lord, do not be far from them. You are their strength, you come quickly to help them," Psalm 22:19. Help each woman press into You for the strength to make it through. And one day soon they will experience the joy of You.

You have given instructions throughout Scripture about the care of widows. We have a special place in Your heart. You will not let us be destroyed by this loss. Your Word says in Exodus 22:22, "Do not take advantage of the widow or the fatherless. If you do and they cry out to me, I will certainly hear their cry."

You sustain the widow. Alone and in need, she places her hope in You. You know her, and You provide all she needs as she cries out.

Chapter Ten

Helpful Books

W hen I searched for a book, sermon, or another woman's testimony of how she dealt with her husband's death, I found
a host of resources for widows.

However, the content predominantly focused on how to live grief
daily, suffering, an aching heart, the agony of loss, and when tears
turn into rivers. I didn't find much that was uplifting or included
forward movement.

Then, my cousin sent me the audio version of *Option B: Facing
Adversity, Building Resilience, and Finding Joy* by Sheryl Sandberg.
At last, I could identify with this author's emotions and decisions she
needed help to make. Even in her agony which described my agony,
she provided hope that there was a way to the other side of grief.

I bought the book to have it at my fingertips. This book helped me
more than any I had read. My husband's death and her husband's
death were both sudden. Neither she nor I knew the first thing to do
for help emotionally, physically, and financially. We both wanted and
needed our husbands. They were the ones who made us feel safe by
handling adversity.

For every widow reading this book, you must find a way to move on. The loss of your husband may paralyze you initially, but you can and will move beyond today.

I hope this book and others give you added strength and perseverance to move forward. You are not alone. I would love to come alongside to aid and equip you.

Personally, I don't like to journal. But I managed to follow a guided journal and jot down my thoughts. This interactive resource, titled, *The Not Just a Widow Guidebook: A Widow's Guide To Surviving Her New Reality And Transforming Into Her New Self* by Patty Desiderio and Doug Robinson, had exercises that went right to the heart of grief and helped explore my sadness. Because my husband and I never got a chance to say goodbye, there were painful mind games that I entertained as a result. Journaling as well as writing this book helped change my perspective around my husband's death. I had felt so angry that he did not listen when I asked him to postpone his trip and seek immediate medical help. He died three days later while on vacation.

These titles brought me needed insights.

- *I Wasn't Ready to Say Goodbye: A Companion Workbook for Surviving, Coping, and Healing After the Sudden Death of a Loved One* by Brooke Noel and Pamela Blair

- *Grace for the Widow: A Journey Through the Fog of Loss* by Joyce Rogers

- *Widow to Widow: Thoughtful, Practical Ideas for Rebuild-*

ing Your Life by Genevieve David Ginsburg

- *Moving Forward on Your Own: A Financial Guidebook for Widows* by Kathleen Ruhl

- *The End of The Beginning* by Julia Lawton

Chapter Eleven

Important Things To Do After Your Spouse Dies

I would call it ironic, but God is all-knowing. He is Omniscient. The fact that I found documents on my husband's computer on things to know when your spouse dies was no coincidence.

My husband was an elder and assistant pastor in our church. He counseled many people on various topics including the death of a spouse. To find on his computer a financial checklist of what to do when your spouse dies was another sign that God was already looking out for me.

Although I found the list a month later, the advice was helpful and pertinent as I tried to make sense of this new stage in my life.

1) Get someone reliable and trustworthy to help you. It is an arduous and overwhelming task to balance things that must be done while grieving.

2) Locate his will if he has one. The will identifies the executor of his estate.

3) Call your attorney for any legal and financial considerations.

4) Contact the Social Security Administration to apply for survivor benefits. They will ask for his Social Security Number and date of birth.

5) If you receive his Social Security check after he dies, you must return the check.

6) You are entitled to receive his Social Security check based on the rules for your individual state. I lived in West Virginia and could collect when I turned 65 and 2 months of age. I was 62 when Al died. If your social security is less than his, you will receive his social security. Social Security will require an original copy of his death certificate.

7) You can report your husband's death online at SSA.Gov There is a lump sum death payment available of $255. This payment has to be claimed with the Social Administration. Details of how to claim can be found at https://www.ssa.gov/forms/ssa-10.html

8) If your husband was employed, contact the Human Resources department at his work as well as his immediate boss.

9) Find out if your husband had a pension. Ask the human resources department where he worked how the pension plan is structured.

10) Call previous employers. He may have a pension from a previous job.

11) If your husband was a Veteran, contact the Veterans Administration. Their online access is www.va.gov

12) Contact all of his insurance holders including life insurance and health insurance. Ask for hard copies of claims and forms.

13) Call the local probate office and arrange to speak with a probate clerk who establishes and implements all probate records, deeds, assignments, and other legal items for recording. This person is usually at the Fiduciary Court, which handles the formal legal process of validating a deceased individual's will. They will specify what paperwork they need and outline fees for services.

14) Go to the county recorder to change titles on all properties.

15) If you do have joint bank accounts, this will become a challenge for you.

16) Contact the three major credit bureaus to get an idea of what money he owes and what accounts are open in his name. The three main credit bureaus are Equifax, Experian, and TransUnion.

17) Contact your CPA. Whether you filed taxes jointly or married but separately, your taxes will need to be paid.

18) Seek help from a financial advisor you can trust to help set up or update your financial plan. You need to know how much money you have and what bills you must pay.

19) If you have children in college, it would be helpful to notify the financial aid office. It is possible that your child may qualify for assistance.

20) Prepare for changes in income. If your husband had life insurance when he died, this will be helpful to cover a lost income. If he did not, his salary is gone. You may be eligible for survivor's benefit in the form of his social security check. Your age will dictate how much you will receive and when you will receive it.

21) Assess your overall liquidity before selling your home to see if this will help financially. A financial planner can help you decide.

22) When possible, wait a year before making big decisions like selling your home. The shock of such an immense life change makes it difficult to make good decisions.

Chapter Twelve

Tangible Tips

I rarely ask anyone to do anything for me.

In hindsight, there were times I could have used a meal, not because I could not afford to buy it, but because I was not in a good place to do my normal daily activities of living. I wondered if something medical was wrong with me. Anemia? Cancer? My heart?

My primary care physician diagnosed depression. Despite a bachelor's degree in Psychology, I did not recognize that I felt depressed. Concerned for my well-being after suffering such an unexpected loss, my doctor prescribed antidepressant meds.

I filled the prescription but never opened the bottle. Rather than deaden the pain, I wanted to walk through the pain so it would be over.

Don't Be Too Proud To Ask For Help

Since my nature is to give rather than receive help, it was very hard for me to admit when I needed someone to give me a hand.

Some of you will not want anyone to think you are not able to handle any kind of adversity that comes your way. Even the sudden or prolonged death of your husband.

There were nights when I reached for that bottle of antidepressants, only to decide that if I could fall asleep naturally, thinking positive thoughts and listening to meditations about God, the next day may be different. My husband used to say life looks different after sleep. Thank God for bringing sleep. When I awoke, I had lived another day.

For some, taking antidepressants may be beneficial. Do not let anyone tell you what is best for you. Don't be embarrassed if antidepressants are needed for a season. This is your life and no one experiences the death of their husband the same way. Seek advice from your primary care physician about what length of time is recommended.

If you cannot eat or sleep, or feel that life is not worth living, see your doctor immediately. Be honest with your medical team so you can get the help you need.

When you have a need, ask for help. Make that phone call to a trusted friend. Allow others to assist with childcare. Accept to another pair of hands to help with a task. Allow someone to offer a shoulder while you cry.

There were times people volunteered their help and I politely told them that I was okay. But I was not. One lady said God had asked her to be helpful. God is at work in the lives of the giver and the receiver. Accept kindnesses with gratitude. You discover the blessing of receiving as the other person experiences the blessing of giving.

The more you let people into your life, the more you find that people are eager to do something. They can't take away the hurt but they can help carry the load.

Recruit a guy friend to do the heavy lifting instead of you suffering through or hurting yourself. Don't be ashamed or too prideful to call your mother, sister, or friend to be with you on a rough day.

Sing When You Can't Speak

I was accustomed to talking to my husband.

He would say jokingly, "You haven't used up all your words yet?"

After his death, the house was empty.

Singing took my mind off the obvious. From gospel to country to music from the 60s, 70s, and 80s, I sang at the top of my lungs.

Sometimes a gospel song made me cry. When the lyrics of the song reminded me that I was not alone in a song such as *You Are For Me* by Kari Jobe, the tears were therapeutic.

God knew we would shed tears at the loss of our husbands. "You keep track of all my sorrows. You have collected all my tears in your bottle. You have recorded each one in your book," Psalm 56:8 NLT.

Perhaps He waters us with those caught tears when we can't cry anymore. He knows what we need before we ask. He has all the provisions.

Find Your Village

Even if you are without overt sadness, some people will not be able to handle your grief. Some will not come around as they once did.

At the exact time you need their presence, you will experience their absence.

Some friends will say insensitive words. "Are you still grieving? Hasn't it been a year since he died?"

Don't answer.

Thank them and walk away. They do not know what it's like to lose a husband.

Even if they have had a similar experience, each person grieves differently.

Find a group of women, some of which may include other widows who know how you feel, that are sincere about your brokenness, and genuinely care about you. They are priceless. They understand when you are in tears with a snotty nose one day, and are praising God the next.

Don't Be Surprised

After the cards, telephone calls, and text messages cease, you will find you are really alone. Support diminishes. People return to their lives.

Don't hold this normal behavior against them. It does not mean they do not love or care about you. Possibly you did the same thing to a widowed friend. I know I did out of ignorance.

Now I know what this loss feels like. Every time I hear of a woman who lost her husband, I cry for her and what she must feel. Whether I know her or not, I pray for her and reach out if I can.

Our shared experience equips us to empathize.

The Pain Does Get Easier With Time

If I told you that the pain you have now will subside, you would probably say you can't imagine it ever getting better. I promise, the deep hurt will ease if you do your part.

See a counselor, psychologist, or someone well versed at handling loss and grief. This step was the launching pad for me to grab by the throat and choke grief until it subsided.

Exercise Or Walk Three Or More Times Per Week

Walking is a full-body movement that clears the mind so you can think rationally and make the right decisions. Walking burns off some of those emotions that hold you captive. Exercise releases endorphins–chemicals produced by the body to manage stress.

Plus, exercise helps you look better. If you look better, you'll feel better.

Avoid overeating or undereating. Both lead to health problems. This is not the time to lose the control God has given. Lean into being positive even when you don't feel like it. You'll be surprised how much better you will feel.

Laugh

Laughter is good medicine for the mind. A powerful antidote, laughter gets rid of sorrow, sadness, and loneliness faster than anything else. Laughter has healing properties that bring your body back into proper balance.

Look for something to laugh about every day. Whether a movie, something funny someone said, or a comedy show, find any and everything that makes you laugh.

Often, I laughed at myself. One night I put on my pajamas over my pants and blouse. I thought about my mama who had dementia, and the time she stood in her slip, wondering if she was getting dressed or undressed.

"Mama," I said aloud, "I've got one up on you." And I burst into uncontrollable laughter.

Studies show laughter reduces the downward spiral of depression. Similar to the cliché, 'fake it 'til you make it,' even forced laughter releases good hormones and dopamine that give the jump-start you need.

Grief May Not Be Linear

In the process of earning a bachelor's degree in psychology, I learned that the stages of grief were linear: denial, anger, depression, bargaining, and acceptance.

According to my training, someone grieving would go through each emotion in turn. Leave one stage of grief and go to the next.

However, since my husband's death, I experienced each stage multiple times and not always in order. Whether you progress through the stages of grief linearly or not, either way is okay.

To me, grief resembles a pentagram. Bouncing in and out of each stage defined where I was with my husband's death. I lingered between denial and depression for what seemed like ages. Six years after his death, I continued to experience the different stages of grief as they arose.

Resist the temptation to compare your process to the way someone else who has lost her husband grieves. You will have common experiences, yet every woman's journey is unique. For some, depression may linger, weaving in and out when triggered by a song, something someone says, a smell, or anniversary.

As years passed, I thought I had accepted Al's death. But every year, the week leading to, and the date of, his death cause depression. Although I am stronger now, I do not hesitate to call or visit a friend, seek counseling, or take a walk. Purposefully, I do something – anything – that can move me from this stage.

I never really stop grieving. It is the open expression of my thoughts and feelings. It is an essential part of healing. After a while, the pain lessens its intensity. It is similar to what an amputee described. "I miss my leg. I used to grieve for it. But now, I've learned to adjust without it. I am doing so incredibly well, that people are in awe. I've been able to move forward, with new strength and a new vigor for my life."

Rather than be afraid of how you feel, admit your feelings to a trusted friend. Instead of wasting energy to keep up an image that you are strong and have moved forward, allow the intensity of your grief to inform you of how deeply you can feel for yourself and for others.

Grief is a reminder of the deep love in our hearts, placed there by God. When the time comes, we will be able to comfort others. 2 Corinthians says, "Praise be to the God and Father of our Lord Jesus

Christ, the Father of compassion and the God of all comfort, who comforts us in all our troubles so that we can comfort those in any trouble with the comfort we ourselves receive from God."

The Right Time To Remarry

When is the right time to date again? The answer is that the right time is different for each individual.

For me, the time came sooner than expected.

"Sister, you are no longer Mrs. Alford Ottley. You are completely free of that title," my pastor said. "As a single woman now, you are no longer bound by your marriage wows. When Al died, you fulfilled your commitment of until death do we part, and you are now free."

Although I was a widow, it never occurred that being a widow meant I was a single woman. After several days, my pastor's words sank in. I removed my wedding rings, tucked them safely with Al's rings, and vowed to choose a new trajectory for my life.

I went to Kay Jewelers. In the first showcase I spotted a ring that I wear to this day. A brown chocolate LeVian diamond cluster ring fit my finger perfectly and spelled freedom for me to find love again.

Many believe looking forward to dating six months after my husband's death is too soon. Opinions are okay. Just do not pass judgment on a woman who moves forward sooner.

A friend asked, "Are you dating?"

"Yes," I replied. "A man I've known for years is a great companion."

"How long has it been since Al died?"

"Six months."

She considered, "How soon can a woman look for companionship after her spouse dies? Six months, a year, or two years?"

"Traditionally," I said, "after one year."

"Whose tradition?"

"That's a good question," I replied. "I don't know. It's just what I have always heard."

"Men are different," my friend observed. "They do not want to be alone, and commonly seek a mate shortly after their wife dies. Why should the rules be different just because you're a woman?"

"In my experience," I shared, "when a widow dates after the loss of her husband should be God-directed instead of man-driven."

"Perhaps women feel dating prior to a year dishonors their husbands. But you could meet the very person God has prepared for you in your new season and miss the opportunity if you're living by a rule." She added, "Your husband is dead. How could finding companionships bring dishonor to him?"

For some widows, dating is the furthest thing from their minds. They had not considered it nor removed their wedding rings. Some will not remarry. Others will.

Some people will judge when you date soon after losing a spouse. Others will not. Rather than focus on what others think, live according to God's guidance for you. You and God make the decision best for you.

When you have experienced the loss of your spouse, that trauma clouds your mind, body, and soul. Making clear, rational decisions is difficult, maybe impossible until you adjust to the shock.

Take life one day at a time before you decide to date or remarry. You do not want to carry trauma into a new relationship. Neither do you want to be the vulnerable victim of false intentions from a man.

I believe it is important to have a signed prenuptial agreement if you choose to remarry. If you have children, you want to protect what you have to offer them. This agreement preserves the family identity. If he doesn't agree to a prenuptial agreement, then you have your answer whether he is the right one.

Be patient. Wait to hear from God. He'll let you know when the time is right to marry or He'll affirm that you are not to remarry at this time. Either decision is good. Be joyful in the decision where God shows is best for you.

Chapter Thirteen

Move Forward

It took me six years to write this book.

Why? Because writing it meant that I would have to remember what I had tried so hard to forget. Every time I started writing, I would cry. I'm crying now as I try to type through tears. Writing this brings to the surface years of struggles, ultimate victories, but mostly his death. When my spouse died, my whole world changed. Writing this book meant I had to recall what it felt like when I first learned of my husband's death. The days, weeks, and months that followed were unbearable. The thought of remembering the details once again was paralyzing.

Nevertheless, I wrote out of obedience to God. He was with me then, and He was with me as I recalled all the things He brought to my remembrance.

I wrote this book because I am convinced that I am not an island in my pain. What I experienced when my husband, Al, died is most likely felt by other widows.

Sometimes I felt numb. Other times I was speechless. I cried buckets and buckets of tears. Death. It does sting.

This book is God's gift from me and the ten widows who contributed. Treasure what resonates. Ignore anything that does not pertain to you.

My only wish is that you would have read this before your husband died. In hindsight, I wish I had been better prepared. But who wants to read such a book when you don't need the content? When my husband died, I needed a plan for how to move forward on a daily basis. I wanted to know how to get a handle on my finances. Mostly, I was desperate to know how to live without him.

The common bond widows share is we have experienced a major loss. No woman can know this loss without the experience. Knowing allows us to help each other move forward no matter the pace. Some move forward quicker than others by their nature. Others adjust sooner because his death was one you knew would happen because of the type of illness. You just didn't know when it would be. Regardless, the operative words are, move forward.

For you who watched your husband's life slowly ebb, when he died, it must have been both bitter and sweet. Watching your loved one suffer in that deteriorating state is painful and requires a unique courage. As women, we were born to be nurturers and fixers. But his dying was outside your ability to fix. So, you comforted while your own heart ached day after day.

You watched him die twice; die from the man he once was, and ultimately his physical death. The shared suffering was exhausting. As a couple, you shared much with each other, even death.

For those gripped by unexpected loss or tragedy, I'm sorry. Losing your husband suddenly is the most rugged. No warning. One moment he is alive, and the next he exists no more. In this situation there is no closure. You did not get to say goodbye, ask for forgiveness, make amends, or tell him how much you dearly loved him.

"If only" replays frequently in the months and years to come. Because that is my experience, I ask you not to dwell on what you will never have the chance to redo. Time is precious and not to be wasted on the "if only." Do not give permission for the "if onlys" to steal from you.

You can let the death of your husband paralyze you, or you can find the strength to move forward. The first step is acknowledging that you are here. Even in the midst of this pain, God is at work.

Put aside comparison to anyone else. The death of your spouse carries memories shared between the two of you. Now, the making of memories with him has ceased. And you will make new memories.

The four grandchildren born since my husband's death will never experience having both grandparents influencing their lives for the Lord. The hard and cold fact is that how I envisioned life growing older with my husband was not in God's plan. Obviously, God knew when my husband would die. He knew my plans for my senior years with Al would never come to fruition.

God has the strength that you and I need to step into the chapter of our new lives without our husbands.

Your husband's death, your grief, and the emotional and physical changes you undergo may seem insurmountable. It will get better.

You will be able to take baby steps at first. Eventually, just like me, you will walk without falling down.

I accept the sorrow of my loss. God teaches and comforts me through His Word. This book is for the women who will lose their husbands now and in the years to come.

In all situations, God is faithful and trustworthy. You did not know death would come for your husband, but God knew. He knows and sees all. He is Jehovah Roi, the God who sees everything that pertains to you and me.

No longer married, you are a widow. A new chapter awaits. I believe it will be a great chapter. Today, figuratively write the first sentence of your new life. A life that does not include your husband, but a new life nevertheless that will include countless people who have been waiting to meet you as well as those who have watched the season you have lived.

There will be an innumerable number of widows waiting to hear how you were able to move forward in the wake of something so devastating as the death of your husband.

To think that God could take such sorrow and turn it into dancing is incomprehensible. But He did it for me and the other ten women. He'll do no less for you.

Chapter Fourteen

God is the Strength of My Life: Sarah's Story

My husband swiped a dollop of icing from the cake and tasted it.

"Hey," my nine-year-old daughter protested.

He rolled his eyes with exaggerated appreciation. "This is the best cake I've ever eaten."

She grinned, pleased with her daddy's praise. "I made it for Father's Day tomorrow."

He leaned near my mother who had come to visit for a couple of weeks. "Hope I feel better tomorrow than I do today."

"You've not been feeling well?" My mom looked at him with sympathy. "Maybe you have the flu."

"I have an appointment to see the doctor on Monday," he noted.

My mother patted his shoulder. "Why don't you go rest."

He nodded and went to the parlor. Minutes later, I followed to check on him. Sitting in his chair, his feet were propped on the coffee table, and he appeared to have dozed off.

He had rested all day, had dinner with the family, and tasted the icing on the cake. Now, I looked closer. His eyes and mouth were wide open. Fear jolted through my body.

"Mom," I called. "Come here."

She came to my side. "What's up?"

I gently closed my husband's eyes. "I believe he's dead."

My mom quickly began CPR. She blew air into his body while I telephoned 9-1-1. My second call was to the next-door neighbor.

Both arrived quickly. The paramedics worked hard to restore my husband's heartbeat, but I already knew he was gone. They rushed him to the hospital. No one could ride in the ambulance, so the neighbor stayed home with my four young children while my mother and I drove to the hospital.

The doctor ran a battery of tests. "Your husband died of a coronary thrombosis," he explained. "I'm sorry for your loss."

The time of death was listed as 10:30 p.m. on June 20.

Earlier, my 12-year-old son had gone shopping with his father. "Daddy is not feeling well," my son observed.

I asked, "Why do you say that?"

"Because," he reasoned, "he had his belt off and pants unbuckled."

I made an appointment for my husband to have a check-up.

"I think you are stressed," the doctor diagnosed, "because of the work you do as a salesman and floor manager." The physician pre-scribed four pills, one to be taken every six hours. He arranged for my husband to be admitted to the hospital for observation.

But instead of returning for observation, my husband was rushed to the hospital in an ambulance. The emergency room doctor pronounced him dead.

Shocked by disbelief, I lingered in the hospital for hours. Reluctant to leave, I remained near him. As morning dawned, I dreaded telling the children.

When my mom and I arrived home from the hospital, my seven-year-old son was outside on the swing. Before I had the chance to say anything to the children, my son spoke.

"Maw Maw," he said to his grandmother, "I can see an angel in the car with daddy."

Though only twelve years old, my oldest boy seemed to understand and stood by my side at the graveside. Later, he took me to visit people which eased my grief.

At the graveside, the CEO of the international company where my husband worked said, "I killed that man. He was under so much pressure at work." The next year, the CEO died.

I had to return to work right away. For a year, I had taught English in middle school and senior high. My students and my family needed me. Though my mother had come for a two-week visit, she never left me after Mark died.

Despite the fact that people were always talking about my husband and the differences he made, the mention of his name brought sadness and the reality that he was gone and never coming back. At the same time, I felt good that they did want to talk about him. I realized that talking about him helped them too.

After my husband died, I taught for 28 years and retired at age 60. When my mother became ill, I took a temporary leave of absence to care for her.

My mother had a tubal pregnancy when I was a child. As a result, though I always wanted siblings, I was an only child. When she died at age 87, I thought back and wondered what I would have done without her. Though relatives said they would help, I never saw them. Only my mother was there to comfort and support me.

I attended a widow's group for three months which helped emotionally but was a constant reminder that these widows were overwhelmed with grief. By immediately accepting the loss of my husband, I focused on the future rather than living in the past.

God was my co-pilot all the way. Experience proved over and over that God continued to provide for me through my children, pastor, and friends. It was the will of God that He took my husband, knowing that I had four young children to raise. I made it because God said I was going to make it and I believed Him. My career in education helped. I spent a lot of time teaching, so I did not spend a lot of time thinking about my loss. I wanted to teach as long as I could.

My husband remains forever in my heart. I will never ever forget him. One student wanted me to date her father after his wife died. She invited him to an event and later asked why he had not asked me to go on a date.

"I don't want to put her through what I'm going through, and what my wife went through," he replied. "I'm an alcoholic."

The pressures of life are grueling. I found it important to surround myself with people who care, like a best girlfriend and people from the neighborhood, work, and church. Sometimes I attended the social events that my husband and I used to attend. We did everything together, so I maintained many of those same activities. Some couples included me in invitations after my husband died. Sometimes people just didn't know what to say.

"If there is anything I can do to help," people would say, "just call."

I didn't know what I needed but appreciated people checking on me. I felt helped when people showed up and just did in as many ways as possible without asking. My husband's company offered to pack me up and send me back home free of charge. People seemed to want to help. Maybe because they saw that I was moving forward as I cared for my children and worked a job.

After my husband died, I always kept him in my heart, even though he was not physically with me. Keeping busy and helping others also helped me find what was normal for me. I joined another group of widows that helped me very much. The women in this group do not remarry. There does not seem to be a need to do so.

Whether a woman should marry after a year or six months, I think that's up to the woman and how God leads her. It would be a shame to miss out on God's blessing in His time frame. Men, on the other hand, have a need for a woman more than a woman has a need for a man. Men prefer private things like sex and having someone to care for them. Women don't seem to have the need quite as strong.

The advice I would give to widows is that assisting others helps you spend less time thinking about yourself. Rather than sit and grieve, get up and become involved in making connections with others. This is good for you because you need other people and they need you. I've done 70 eulogies for widows because it is helpful for the widow and the guests and the family.

You may want to sell your house or make the home look different. I left everything the same in the house.

My kids would say, "That's Daddy's chair."

"Yes," I agreed. "You can sit there if you like."

Only two years old when his daddy died, our youngest child doesn't remember him at all. One of my children was killed at the age of 45 in a crop duster plane in Arkansas. Not having him in my life was very different, but I never changed even a picture of my husband or children in the house where we lived.

I recommend widows give themselves permission to cry. Let the tears roll. Seek spiritual counseling. For six months I counseled with my pastor and with hospice.

Gain independence. I took care of the children, and I did substitute teaching. I handled the bills and everything around the house. My husband made the money, and together we took care of the needs of our family.

When I was 30 years old, my husband taught me how to drive. He was an outstanding teacher. My sister-in-law took me to get my license. On our way, I saw children playing and drove very slowly. Noticing cars going in the same direction on both sides of the street, I realized I had turned the wrong way on a one-way street.

"I'm sorry," I said to the police officer who pulled me over. "I'm on my way to get my license, but I think I just failed my driver's test."

"You passed," he said, "because you were being so careful around the children."

I learned to expect that people are human, and sometimes they can say the wrong things with the intent to console. When my husband died, some well-meaning people said, "He's in a better place."

I hate that statement. We don't know whether people are in a better place or not. We can hope and look forward to that place ourselves. I thanked them for their concern and for trying to help me feel better. Maybe the reason they said that my husband was in a better place was that saying those words made them feel better.

People don't always feel comfortable around a widow. A lot of people felt uncomfortable about me talking about my husband. Although I was comfortable, I respected their being uncomfortable and I did not talk about him.

Some widows do not do well with their husband's death. Some women want to die too. I had four children who needed me. I wanted to live each moment of my life to the fullest. I'm grateful to be alive because God planned my life, knowing my husband would not be with me. At age 95, I can shift my thoughts, look back without regrets, and focus on the good.

Chapter Fifteen

Not Unto Your Death But To My Glory: Cindy's Story

Experiencing congestive heart failure, Chas arrived at the emergency room where the ER doctor, a friend, waited.

Diagnosing three clogged arteries, the medical team immediately transferred Chas to another hospital. Three weeks later, he had open heart surgery. In addition to this procedure, Chas developed appendicitis.

After his open-heart surgery, the healing extended to seventeen months. He never fully recovered. A robust man, full of life and vigor, his health ebbed and the process was painful to watch.

At last hospice came to tend my husband at home.

"He has passed," said the hospice nurse. She moved to take off the oxygen.

"No," I said. "He might not be gone."

She offered her stethoscope and I listened. There was no heartbeat. I remained in the room until the changes in his body made me uncomfortable. Even a decade later, I could remember the events of his death as if it had just occurred.

Although the loss felt extremely hard, I cannot imagine going through without the support of my two daughters, son-in-law, and five grandchildren. They helped me accept the initial realization that he was dead.

I received support from my friend and contractor who lived down the street. For that first year, he stopped by daily to check on me, have a beer, and chat. I did not realize how much those visits during this time meant until one day I was all alone. No one consistently stopped by ever again.

Without my husband – my cheerleader – I had no interest in working on my business for nearly two years after he passed. Though I had seventeen months to prepare and accept that this was going to happen, I spent three months in the isolation stage of grief.

I felt bad that I moved on faster than Chas's best friend and family, yet I had been his caretaker for seventeen months. I accepted that he was not coming back. Chas is finally home.

Though there is comfort in knowing he is with God, his absence sometimes led me to grieve my loss of him. I could not tell him when I won an award or when our new great-grandchild was born. He had always been the first to know everything that happened in my life.

I wrote this letter to Chas, releasing those places of pain, and but not ever say goodbye to him:

My dearest Chas,

Thank you for being the best husband for 25 years a woman could have. You've been a fantastic dad and grandfather. A man's man and a woman's man, and the greatest man I have ever known.

After five years of friendship, I was honored to become your wife. I praise God for that daily. I have never had anyone love me as completely as you did.

We were blessed to spend our final week saying our goodbyes to each other, to family, and close friends. Speaking the things we wanted to say to one another were precious days that I will always treasure. Thank you for releasing me to family and close friends, and your encouragement for me to find love again.

Losing you was rough. Mostly I missed you at night. Each day I had a good cry with our poodle, Nikki. He had actual tears in his eyes too. He missed you so much.

A few days after you were gone, as I drove to 7-11, it hit me, "I am no longer married." What a horrible realization. Satan taunted me with the Scripture, "till death do you part."

The worst day was when Troy took your clothes, shoes, and belongings and gave them to men in need. As he drove away, I felt exactly like I did six weeks earlier when the funeral home took away your body. So final.

Before I was able to rebound, I fell back into some old habits. I started smoking seventeen months before you died and was a closet smoker to everyone except my family. Spending money didn't ease my heartbreak. Dinner was often a cheese stick and wine. Because I didn't have an appetite, I lost so much weight that I needed a new wardrobe. Even when friends took me out to eat, I wanted my husband to take me to dinner as he always did. But no matter how hard I wished, that would never happen again.

Were these behaviors because I was so grief-stricken? Or were you such a light to me that I did not want to disappoint you when you were alive? I realized I did not want to disappoint me as a result of your death.

Some widows want to die themselves. I did not feel as though I wanted to die, I just did not care. I wanted to be left alone to smoke my cigarettes and process. Seventeen months after you passed, I quit smoking.

Buying plants without you on the first of May brought tears. Each first without you made me cry; your birthday, Thanksgiving, and Christmas, the first anniversary of your death.

Watching women become stuck in grief, I knew you did not want that for me, and I did not want it either. I was determined not to get stuck. Instead, I leaned on the promise that I did not grieve like someone who did not know where you are.

Two years later, I married another wonderful guy who looks forward to meeting you in heaven. You will like him, Honey, everyone does.

Periodically, missing you sweeps over me. "God," I pray, "tell him hello, that I love him and miss him, and will see him soon." You get those messages because I immediately feel better.

I know you are having a blast, and I look forward to seeing my brother and fellow saint in heaven. Together we can rock out praises to our King. Until that day, I hold close in my heart these fond memories of us.

I love you so much,

Cindy

I promised Chas I would finish and publish his book to give to family and friends. For four years, the manuscript waited for me to be able to begin the task. I worked on it during a cruise, and plan to finish to keep my word.

No longer having the person that meant everything in my life felt like an overwhelming void. I know people meant well, but some things they did were irritating. Frequent phone calls to ask what I needed only disturbed me. Some tried to get me into a women's prayer group. Others dropped by to see how I was doing but stayed much longer than I needed them to stay.

I did not really know what I needed because I felt extremely numb. I wanted to be left alone for the first few months, except for family and a few close friends.

I do not like crying in front of people that I am not close to. When those who were not very involved in our lives wanted to give condolences and call every month, their actions only reminded me of how affected I felt not having Chas near. When people popped in who were our friends, that did not hurt nearly as bad.

Then dinner dates happened again with my new husband. I am thankful I let my heart love again instead of mourning my life away.

I do not think any widow should wait a year or more before experiencing dating, companionship, or even marriage to a man that desires her and wants to show her a good time. If a man is willing to wine and dine her, take her on cruises, or spend time holding hands, it's her decision. The timeframe for when a woman moves on with her life will be unique to her.

For seventeen months, I grieved for the life I knew we were not going to share. Chas and I agreed that no major financial decision like moving or selling the house should be made for at least a year. But Chas also told me he wanted me to truly love again whenever love came my way, no matter the timing.

I would feel the same way about Chas loving again if I had died first. If God brings love, consider welcoming the gift. You are not married anymore, and life is for the living.

To clear the initial Widow's Brain Fog, after some time alone, I got out of the house to socialize and shop for new clothes. It was an adjustment not to answer to anyone. Eventually, I laughed aloud again.

If I could give other widows advice, I would say, don't rush the process. Feel what you feel but do not become stagnant nor grieve too long. Life is for the living. You are no longer married anymore and therefore you are not cheating on him.

Surround yourself with family and friends. Learn to have fun, laugh again, and just maybe love again.

Do not be embarrassed to go to counseling. I got into an online grief group, but their timelines for what could not be done until a year or two felt hindering. Listening to those in the grief group tell how empty their lives were without their husbands, I fell back into a funk. As I began to press forward, I left the group.

Give yourself permission to grieve, but do not let grief consume you. Do not be surprised when the couples you and your husband socialized with become scarce. They do not know what to say or how to support you. The people you considered your best friends who you thought would be present for you, are experiencing their own grief.

If you want to talk about your husband, engage those that enjoy hearing about him. Everybody may not want to reminisce, but there are those who long to hear you talk about him so they can talk about him too. My heart is warmed when friends and family talk about Chas.

My daughter's new in-laws were uncomfortable with me talking about Chas because of my new hubby, but my new husband likes hearing about Chas. Perhaps people who are divorced do not want to think or talk about ex-spouses because of the pain involved. But the situation is different when a spouse dies. If I dated someone who did not like my friends, family, or me talking about Chas, that would be a deal-breaker.

Chapter Sixteen

God Showed Me His Grace and Love: Betty's Story

P lagued by increasing physical problems, Will suffered greatly in the final two years of his life.

As his health declined, he required round-the-clock care. When providing full time care for my husband grew more strenuous and stressful, we relocated so that I could have the help and support of our adult daughter.

For 24 years, his body struggled with one illness after another. Each left him more debilitated. He experienced diabetes, heart rhythm issues, nerve damage, problems throughout his digestive system, and he received dialysis. He fought a life-threatening bacterial infection and survived two strokes.

Then he had a third stroke.

"Call 9-1-1," I instructed my grandson.

The operator asked if we heard any sounds of breathing or gasping for breath. My grandson counted Will's respirations. As I held Will, there came a few gasps, then his breathing stopped. My husband died in my arms.

The EMT service arrived quickly. They tore off his clothes and started doing procedures to bring him back. Moving fast, they took him into the ambulance.

At the small, local hospital, the medical team put my husband on the respirator and other machines. A brain scan reported there was no brain activity.

He was taken by ambulance to a hospital outside of Leesburg, Virginia. The doctor there confirmed Will was brain dead.

When I saw his chest rise and fall, I thought he was breathing somewhat on his own. But the doctor explained that with no brain activity, he could not live without the support of the ventilator.

My daughter and son-in-law prayed with me about the decision that had to be made. I prayed in faith that if God wanted to heal my husband again, he could. An hour later, I decided to take him off life support. I felt peace that this was the right thing to do.

I thank God for my family. My daughter, son-in-law, and grandchildren were there to provide support. One arranged to leave work, another took time from college, but each found a way to be near. My grandson who lived a longer distance away came for the funeral.

Thanksgiving and Christmas that year were particularly hard. We had to wait until after the holidays to hold the memorial service so people could come.

After the funeral, two close friends came to stay with me. Both were licensed Christian counselors. They stayed two to three days each time and phoned often in between. They invited me to visit them in Richmond whenever I wanted.

One friend had lost her husband five years earlier. She understood what I was going through and offered consolation. My pastor sent three books about grieving. I joined a widow's group.

For five days I stayed with a friend who cared for her husband who had dementia. Though caretaking brought back painful memories, knowing that I provided support for her helped me. Helping others helped me.

Will and I had relocated often because of his job. Now I had to get health insurance because I had become the main breadwinner.

My friends would ask to come over. I appreciated their thoughtfulness. We chatted and had dinner at one another's home. But with all their support, the worst time came in the evening. Even being absorbed in activity until I became sleepy, the night was a constant reminder that my husband was not by my side. In those last years, each night after dinner we listened to an audiobook or watched a movie and listened to the news. We looked forward to those moments because that was all he could do anyway.

Even with supportive family, and friends who could stay over, no one could fill the empty space in my heart that longed for my husband.

Will died a week before Thanksgiving. That holiday was the first reality check that he would no longer join our family for celebrations. The first few weeks were flooded with great sadness. Depression comes and goes, and is particularly felt during holidays, birthdays, and anniversaries.

My joy came when people volunteered and just did things for me. I was in a fog for months and making decisions felt impossible. Normally, I am decisive and organized. When my husband became ill, I took over the finances, banking, paying the bills, and investing. In hindsight, I see this was a blessing.

One friend didn't realize her husband's dementia was so bad that he had not paid bills for six months. They were about to lose their home. The water and electricity were about to be shut off. Previously, her husband took care of everything. Now that he was sick, she didn't know the passwords to their accounts.

With my spouse gone, I needed time to understand who I was without him. I needed to think and pray.

God knew I needed my Sunday School teacher. A retired missionary, she ministered in Brazil for 33 years. She was instrumental in helping put the pieces of my life in perspective. Two weeks after my husband died, she dreamed she was in heaven talking face-to-face with Will.

"He leaped, sang, and danced with joy," she described.

Her dream was a comfort, affirming that my husband is happier than he ever experienced on this earth. Pleasant to be around, Will laughed often. Healed and whole in heaven, he would laugh wholeheartedly.

Her dream brought peace and the freedom to talk about Will. I'd bring up his name when it naturally fit in conversations. This seemed to put others at ease when the words were not forced.

Despite his suffering, Will rarely complained. Missing him, I couldn't fill the void of his absence. Counseling helped with all the emotions that came as a result of my husband's death.

Sometimes, all of a sudden, I would cry. People's love and showering of kindness, seeing God's grace through others brought tears.

When I joined the widow's group, occasionally someone mentioned their husband.

One woman said, "We don't continually talk about our husbands. We have a good time."

I didn't want to cry all the time, nor did I want to go on as if he never existed. The best way I found to combat crying and feeling lonely was to engage in activities I used to do including being a counselor for the crisis pregnancy center, and teaching children at church to worship through song. Getting together with friends was possible now that my husband no longer needed my consistent care.

The more I allowed God to work His plan in my life, even the very difficult, hard, and sad things, the more my trust in Him grew. As I moved forward into the next chapter of my life without my husband, I began to heal.

I tell widows they will face hard times, but don't despair. Open yourself to healing and joy by letting people and the church show their love. People close themselves off when they're in pain and grief. Feeling negative, we don't want to talk to, or see, anybody. But such unhappiness gets worse unless we let it go. We were born to be in communion. Being with others gives the chance to heal.

Chapter Seventeen

To God Be the Glory: Pamela's Story

My husband, Brandon, noticed numbness in three of his fingers on his left hand and our family doctor sent him to a specialist. On April 15, 2008, the neurologist diagnosed carpal tunnel.

I felt the problem was connected to a problem in his brain, but the doctor refused an MRI.

While at work one day, my husband felt his eye jump up and down in his head. He phoned his doctor who prescribed seizure medicine. The seizure drug caused him to sweat profusely so he stopped taking it.

I suggested we get a second opinion, but my husband liked the doctor and wanted to know the results of other tests the doctor had ordered. Brandon's health declined. On October 10, 2008, my husband's appearance concerned me.

"Get your toothbrush, razor, and pillow," I instructed. "I'm taking you to the Emergency Room and I'm sure you won't be coming home with me."

We told our college-age daughter, who lived at our home with her two small children, we were going to the hospital. On our way, we phoned our son and he met us at the ER.

The ER was packed with patients waiting to be seen. At the registration window, they handed us paperwork to fill out. One of the questions asked the reason for seeking medical attention.

I looked at Brandon. "What do I write?" I settled on "numbness."

Brandon's name was called. Seeing the seriousness of the situation, the medical team put him on a heart monitor, took five vials of blood, and ordered an MRI.

The doctor spoke with us about the test results. "Brandon has stage four glioblastoma."

The diagnosis came as a shock. I tried to ask a question, but no words came. I took my son's hand and noticed he was shaking uncontrollably.

Brandon's tumor was the size of a large egg. Brandon was immediately given seizure medicine to prevent a grand mal that could occur at any moment.

The next morning Brandon said, "Before I went to sleep, I prayed, 'Lord, in Your Word You said that You give peace that passes all understanding. If that is true, I need it and I need it now." He continued, "Before I finished speaking, peace came. I asked Him, "Can we talk about everything and anything" and He replied "Yes."

After several days, the doctor gave the option of going home while they put together a team for Brandon's surgery. We chose to go home so Brandon could be with our children and grandchildren.

On Wednesday, October 15th, Brandon returned to the hospital. His brothers and sisters, their spouses, and our church family filled the waiting room. Pastors from two churches prayed with us. In the waiting room, our group prayed, talked, prayed, and took short walks.

Following surgery, two doctors reported that Brandon did well. The tumor appeared contained. Relieved, family and friends went home. I remained close, staying in a home provided by the hospital for families in situations like ours.

But the following morning, Brandon's left side was paralyzed. During the next few days, the social worker arranged for Brandon to go to a rehab facility where the technicians were encouraging and his roommate was easy for Brandon to talk with.

A month after surgery, the surgeon reported Brandon's brain was clear of new glioblastomas. We decided to go ahead with chemo and radiation as the doctor recommended.

That evening at home, Brandon sat in a handicap chair in the bathtub while I washed his hair. He asked me to wait so he could catch his breath. But instead of exhaling, his stomach grew large.

My eight-year-old grandson heard me call for help and ran to tell his mother to call 911.

I couldn't lay Brandon down and I didn't know how to do CPR with someone sitting up. Nervousness, I struck him with an open hand across the chest. He gasped for air.

My daughter brought the phone and the lady on the other end told me to raise his chin. He started breathing.

The EMTs arrived and transported Brandon to our local hospital where they found he had a pulmonary embolism. Brandon was transferred to the hospital that did his brain surgery. While the doctor's instructions were that Brandon be admitted into the Critical Care Unit, the hospitalist felt his case was not that serious and directed he be put on another floor. I advocated for my husband with the decision makers until someone confirmed that his case was serious. Finally, he was admitted to the Critical Care Unit.

My husband remained in the CCU for seven days. In his critical condition, he had no idea of what was going on around him. Following another round of rehab, he started outpatient radiation and chemo.

People offered to help take him to radiation, but he wanted me to be the one. We had sweet moments on the trips to his radiation that I would not have wanted to miss for the world.

Home health drew blood until he became stable on his blood thinners. Physical therapists and occupational therapists taught him to care for himself and helped him increase his strength.

On March 5, he woke up unable to sit up. X-rays revealed three tumors in his right lung. A biopsy confirmed a glioblastoma cancer in his lung. Because he was terminal we said no to more testing.

Years before, Brandon and I had talked about dying. We wanted to be home where the setting felt familiar and family could come and go.

On Monday, I brought Brandon home under hospice. Family and friends visited until he was no longer able to communicate with us. To ease his increasing pain, the morphine was increased until

84

Brandon could no longer communicate. He lived at home for nine days.

I slept on the couch behind Brandon's bed. I woke up around midnight to check on him. My friend checked his heartbeat and said it wouldn't be long.

We sat in the room with him, talking in low voices. When he seemed uncomfortable, we stopped talking and he quieted down. A short time later, he passed away.

Brandon's family and my children helped with the funeral arrangements. At the viewing, several people told their stories of how their spouse died. This was almost too much, but I listened. That experience taught me that when someone is grieving, I will not tell my story. That is the time to focus on the person who has just lost their spouse.

Thinking back over the years feels like trying to see through thick fog. I grieved hard for two years. I went to lunch with friends, attended church, and watched my grandchildren. Alone, I grieved.

My daughter was in college and grieving. My son worked while dealing with his grief. My family and church family helped tremendously to make this transition in my life.

I had a wonderful marriage, and my husband was my best friend. You can't love and not grieve. The talks we had those five months before his death were healing in my grieving.

I wanted to be in heaven with my husband, but one morning I realized that God wanted me to be here. I decided I needed to take care of myself and start living. God has been faithful, and He's been enough.

Brandon and I were married for 45 years and seven months. My husband took good care of me when he was alive, and I still feel he's taking care of me. He had life insurance, a 401(k), and a pension from his job. His monetary provisions allow me to do the things I love including gardening, mowing, and shoveling snow. I keep busy with my family and church family.

When Brandon died, I never questioned God. God gives life and our days are numbered. I thank Him for the years I was able to be Brandon's wife.

Chapter Eighteen

Waiting For A Miracle: Mary's Story

Diagnosed too late, my husband died of stage-four colon cancer.

The doctor detected the problem in 2011. Chemotherapy and radiation followed but the prognosis was not promising.

An optimist, my husband believed there had to be one more option. Our children accompanied him to his medical appointments. They were present when the final news came.

"There are just too many cancerous spots on the liver," the oncologist said. "There's nothing more we can do."

Warren said he wasn't ready to go, but he accepted the reality. Until the final week of his life, he tried to be a comfort for his children, to get the family reconciled to the fact that he was dying. Even when he looked like he preferred not to see anyone, he welcomed people who wanted to see him. Despite increasing pain, he continued to drive to work.

Two weeks after his medical team said there was nothing more they could do to preserve his life, my husband died. He somehow managed to go to the bathroom without assistance. And the next thing I knew, he fell to the floor and died.

My daughter was visiting. She was a daddy's girl and rarely left his side. I called her to come into the bathroom, and I phoned my son who lived away. I did not want the family to hear from strangers that their father had died.

In the final days of his life, I contacted hospice. While others, including my cousin, found hospice to be helpful, I did not have a good experience.

I called hospice at 5:00 a.m. to say Warren had died. Rather than come to the house to declare him dead, hospice instructed me to call the funeral home. I dialed 911 and emergency personnel came and pronounced him dead based on the time we saw him take his last breath. The police had to get involved because he died at home. This could have been avoided if hospice had been present.

Though the doctor had given a timeframe and there were signs he was not improving, I was unprepared for his death. Though we had known the diagnosis was terminal for four years, we never talked about him dying. Being sickly doesn't mean that person will be the first to die.

He's really gone, I thought. Having held onto hope until I had to let hope go, it was difficult to believe Warren was gone. My daughter cried and I buried my feelings to console her. Life for her, for my son, and for everyone who knew him would forever be altered.

I watched my spouse take his final breath. Some inner strength took over so I could take care of what needed to be done.

My children came by to check on me every weekend and as often as they could. My brother and sisters also came to help.

After some time had passed and everyone moved on with their lives, I began to get in touch with my feelings. Though I accepted Warren's death, I had bouts with depression. That's why I continued to work. I was lonely. I missed him.

I did not want to fill that loneliness with another companion. Sometimes I felt angry when I think of the many things Warren used to do and now those tasks and responsibilities are mine. And I regret the times I nagged him to do this or that around the house.

Our home is paid off though I had problems with the water and other repairs. Many recommended I give up staying in our home because maintenance issues are costly. But where would I go that doesn't have the same problems?

For five years I paid taxes and insurance on cars I didn't drive. The extra vehicles should have been sold as soon as Warren was gone but I put it off. Figuring out how to survive without Warren seemed never-ending. Feeling alone and lonely, isolated and depressed, I moved from one grief stage to another.

Occasionally I visited my aunts or shopped.s I attend church on Sundays. I see my granddaughter every two weeks. Monthly, my sisters and brothers do an online video call that keeps me connected without a visit. But there were times when I longed to have someone just sit and talk with me.

People often don't know what to say, and a few things that were said and done irritated me. Warren had been the head deacon at our church. On any given day someone called and asked for him.

"He isn't here," I replied. "Can I take a message?"

My husband's brother died six months before him. His siblings checked on my sister-in-law regularly. But when Warren died, his brothers did not check on me. That was hurtful. And there were things I needed help with, but I wasn't going to ask.

One brother-in-law volunteered to cut the shrubs. He said if I ever had a man come to my house, he would no longer help. I had the shrubs removed. Holiday traditions we shared with my husband's family immediately changed. I was doubly heartbroken to lose my husband and feel excluded by the in-laws who had been family for more than 30 years.

I liked the idea of people volunteering to help, but when Warren died, people said, "If there is anything you need, just call."

Because I didn't know what I needed, I never called anyone who asked. When someone brought a meal or took me to lunch, it showed they cared.

My two cousins were also widows and we went together to events. Classmates I had not seen in a long time came by. One friend's husband also had cancer which resulted in several surgeries. Because we shared similar experiences, she and I could talk, share, and listen to one another. My circumstances were bad, but others went through worse. While I couldn't truly identify with the intensity of another's loss, we had in common that we experienced the death of our husbands.

I wondered how I would feel with a companion. Each time the thought entered my mind, I said "That's not for me." For each widow, when to date or not to date is up to her and God.

If circumstances had been reversed, Warren would have remarried. His daddy married six months after Warren's mother died. Warren's father married again a couple of months after his second wife died. He was on his way to marrying again in his 80s when he became sick. Unconcerned with what people thought, he lived the way he felt life was to be lived.

I'm not looking to get married, but it was helpful when I changed churches. This was Warren's church and the place where we were married. Experts advise waiting a year before making major changes so I stayed even though I was sad each time I went. Attending was a constant reminder, the feeling that he was there but with each service, I knew he would not show up.

He had been so sick with cancer. He kept up with his church responsibilities until his pain became too severe. Years after he died, I went home after church and ate alone. My feelings of loneliness and depression grew every Sunday, rebounded, and began again on the following Sunday.

Finally, I realized that church was a part of not being able to move forward. One of the best moves I made was to attend a congregation where my relatives went. Having lunch on Sunday afternoons with my cousin and her children was a relief. I wish someone had said it was going to be hard staying at my husband's church.

Conscious of security, I locked up anything I could. To make sure I'm safe, I put up security cameras. One night, someone in the neighborhood was shooting. If that were to continue, I would go. Living close to the woods, I have a professional spray around the house so snakes don't get indoors.

Since my husband's death, so much seems overwhelming. I had people I could talk to, and my job offered a free and confidential counseling program. When I felt depressed, I worked later and came home and went to bed.

Six months before Warren died, his brother died. His wife and I would talk. But when she began dating, we stopped talking as often. Though my sisters are available to chat, when I go to bed at night, I'm alone. That's when I think about how life was and I cry. Warren and I had our differences, but I remember the good times.

People said, "He's in a better place."

I believe Warren is in heaven but only God knows. Perhaps people say such things because they don't know what to say. I probably said it myself. But I'm more conscious of what I say now. People want me to feel better, or maybe they say those words to make them feel better. The sentiment didn't make me feel better. I miss my husband.

Something about shopping helped. Not the best thing I could do with my money but being in the stores gave me a different perspective. Returning home, of course, I was hit with the reality that my husband was not ever going to be there again.

Going from store to store, I bought so much stuff that I needed more space in my closet. Half the closet held his things and half had my things.

"I don't know why you have so much stuff," he would say.

After he died, I took his clothes out of the closet and drawers and filled the space with my clothes. Yes, I fell back into old habits of spending money. But like everything in life, I realized that things don't satisfy or fill a void. Thankfully, I was able to move forward despite the obvious setbacks.

I would advise others to be less reliant on their husband to do everything. Even if you're not paying the bills, learn what is involved. Pay off as much as you can to be in a better financial situation. Expect the unexpected regarding a house. I painted and redid the floors. I hired someone to help but did most of the work myself because I didn't want a lot of folks I didn't know coming into my house.

It's helpful to have family and friends who pitch in, especially if their efforts can save money. But if they don't have the skill set, you're better off paying the first time to have the task done right.

I thank God for my marriage. God provided a good husband, companion, provider, and soulmate for me.

Chapter Nineteen

A Pen in the Hand of God: Sharon's Story

I can hardly believe that it has been two years since Noel died.

We were in Florida on a family vacation. Our daughter's entire family got sick with Covid including myself. When my husband became ill and struggled to breathe, I took him to the hospital.

The ER hospital staff quickly took him back to a room and asked me not to come. That was the last time I saw him. In less than a week after he contracted Covid, he was gone.

I don't know how other women endured such a loss, but when I heard that he died, I passed out from the shock. When I came to myself, all I could feel was numb. He was really gone.

The week that followed his death seemed like a nightmare. I would wake in the middle of the night and relive those pivotal days over and over again. If it had not been for my daughter, her husband, and her family, I don't know what I would have done.

My daughter had just lost her father. I knew what that felt like because I had lost mine when I was a young girl. The pain of losing an icon of a dad hurts more than what can be articulated in words. Nevertheless, she was there for me as much as I was there for her. We knew life must go on.

Teaching piano to my students and caring for other people helped me through the first months. I still give myself to my students, pouring all of me out for them instead of Noel.

At the end of each lesson, when the students went home, I felt extreme loneliness, sadness, and sometimes fear. But I had a purpose for living because God left me here. My students said they excelled beyond my expectations because I cared so much for them. I thank God for giving me the ability to teach music. Teaching piano became my lifeline.

During my lonely periods, which seemed to be most of the time, I concentrated on the good times we had as husband and wife. I wish I had the opportunity again to tell Noel how wonderful he was and how privileged and honored I felt to be his wife. We were a team supporting each other and doing life together. He encouraged my piano teaching and I promoted his ministry to people. I miss him so much.

Since I will never have the opportunity again to say what my heart wants to say to Noel, I wrote him a letter. Because he was taken away so quickly at the hospital, I did not get to say the words I longed to speak to my husband. Somehow, I believe that he will hear what I write in my letter to him.

Dearest Noel,

I want you to know how much your life meant to me. Your listening, caring, and encouragement gave me strength. Coming out of the hurts you experienced as a child, your desire for a close relationship with Jesus impacted me. A gifted communicator of the gospel, your singing ministry touched the lives of many.

You filled my life with security and confidence in my abilities. You were always there for me. I wish I had one more chance to tell you how much I love you. Just one more opportunity to do something special for you. One more time to see you smile.

I wear my wedding rings to honor you. I will always love you and feel a sense of your presence in my life. Thank you for the many messages you left, giving me direction and purpose.

Noel, I am your Lord Christ. I am the Son of God who created you. You belong to me. Will you give me your life for today?

Oh, Lord Christ, in accordance with your command, I give you my life for today. All that I am and all that I have to be totally and unconditionally yours for your use. Take me away from self and use me up, as you will, when you will, where you will, and with whom you will.

Lovingly, your wife Sharon

Without God, I could have never survived when my world was turned upside down. Since I was a child, I have had to depend on Him for strength on dark days. I feel a deeper dependence on Jesus to lead and guide me moment by moment. Colossians 1:27 says, "Christ in me my hope of glory" (NIV).

In a letter to myself, I expressed how I feel now that my husband is gone.

Dear Sharon,

You are living with a hole in your heart despite being thankful for the blessings of having a Christ-centered marriage. You feel you took so many of your blessings for granted. You lived as if life would always continue. There wasn't a fear of death or separation.

Suddenly you were faced with sickness, hospitalization, and not allowed visitation or communication. Within a week your loved one was gone. You were in a state of shock, disbelief, fear, sadness, and complete helplessness. Yet, next to your bed was your husband's list of favorite Bible verses he shared with hurting and seeking people. There was also his cherished book on prayer by Tozer. These became your lifeline to Jesus.

Noel's verse became my verse and continues to point me to the one who gives strength to go on. Deuteronomy 31:8 says "It is the Lord who goes before you. He will be with you. He will not fail you or forsake you. Do not fear or be dismayed," (United States Conference of Catholic Bishops).

As Noel often said, "When you have nothing but God, you will discover He is all you need."

Press into Jesus,

Sharon

That verse became so real in the months and years that have passed. I was alone without my family to support me. My children lived far away. Thank God for the wonderful supportive people in my church, along with the parents of my piano students, and a few good neighbors. Although the first year left me feeling numb, I learned to take life one day at a time. That's what Noel would want me to do. That's what the Lord would have me do. "Therefore do not worry about tomorrow, for tomorrow will worry about itself. Each day has enough trouble of its own, (Matthew 6:34).

I felt it was beneficial to move forward. Having people reach out with support was major. My mother died from an illness the year before. My father had died many years before her. I had no siblings. I longed to be surrounded by people to help fill the void of Noel's absence. Because we had moved away from family, relatives, and close friends in the Midwest, I did not know many people in our new neighborhood on the East Coast. Thankfully, I had 17 piano students who came regularly for lessons.

I believe it is important for widows to stay connected to people. God is still using us for his purposes. But I caution widows when it comes to being connected to a man who may show interest or want to marry them. Major decisions, such as getting married, should wait for at least a year after a husband's death. My ultimate advice is to draw near to God and he will draw near to you as promised in James 4:8, "Come near to God and he will come near to you."

Keeping my surroundings the same helped me sense my husband's presence. If you find it necessary to go to counseling, you should do so. As a pastor's wife, I had received prior training in grief counseling.

Financially, I handled my piano business and my husband took care of everything else. While I have been managing the finances by myself to the best of my ability, this has been a struggle. Sometimes I ask my son who lives in Japan about things I am uncertain about. It is wise to work with a trusted person who is well-versed in finances to help along the way.

I gained so much from my husband's life and faith and all the people he helped. It strengthens me to share how God has used him in my life and in the lives of others. Now I am available to be used in the lives of others. I look to Jesus for strength to keep pressing on. The Bible gives me hope through life's trials. As my husband often said, "When all you have is God, you will discover He is all you need."

Chapter Twenty

Widowhood: Descent into The Abyss of Despair: Monica's Story

M ichael had a longstanding history of acid reflux and Barrett's esophagus, a complication of gastroesophageal reflux disease. Diligent with his medication, doctor's appointments, and annual endoscopies, we thought his condition was controlled.

In September 2005, he had his annual endoscopy. A week later Michael went to work at 8:00 a.m. and I left home mid-afternoon to prepare for my 8:00 p.m. class at the University. When I arrived home that night, Michael sat at the kitchen table. He had prepared something for me to eat and my favorite drink.

I smiled at his thoughtfulness. "How was your day?"

"I have cancer."

"Stop joking," I replied. "That is not amusing."

"The gastroenterologist called. My test results are positive for adenocarcinoma of the esophagus."

I went with him to see the surgeon. The adenocarcinoma was very early, robotic surgery was recommended, and a full recovery was anticipated. Michael would be hospitalized five days, discharged to home, and return to work in 30 days.

"The procedure is difficult but straightforward," the surgeon said. "With robotic surgery, recovery will be much faster with less pain and less blood loss than with traditional surgery."

I suggested a consultation with a specialist in this type of surgery at Memorial Sloan Kettering Medical Center, the renowned cancer institute. But Michael trusted this doctor and felt there was no need for a second opinion. My husband was a smart, educated man, competent, and this was his life.

The morning of the procedure, his surgery was delayed for several hours. Always a calm person, Michael's anxiety increased with every minute of delay. When he was finally taken to the operating room, there was an issue with his blood pressure and an issue with inserting a catheter into his bladder that required the urologist to be called.

When the surgery took several hours, I knew something must have gone wrong. Later, the surgeon said everything went well except for the issues before the start of the surgery.

During the procedure, about five inches was removed from the esophagus as well as the top third of his stomach. What was not recognized prior to his discharge was an anastomotic leak. The suture line that connected the esophagus to the stomach did not hold. This serious complication of resection surgery leads to a high infection and death rate.

A Gastrografin (oral contrast) swallow test was conducted prior to his discharge to make sure there was no leak. Though Michael was in severe pain, the surgeon said everything was fine, and they discharged him.. Two days after discharge, he was doubled over in pain, and I took him back to the hospital emergency room where they identified the anastomotic leak. I learned later that the gold standard test to check for an anastomotic leak was a CAT scan, not a Gastrografin swallow test.

Instead of the doctors immediately doing a second surgery to correct the leak, surgery was scheduled for two days later. I believe they knew they made a mistake; they knew Michael was dying, and they felt nature would take its course and he would die before the surgery.

Michael lived to keep the surgery date. That's when the anesthesiologist explained Michael would remain on the respirator and be transferred to ICU. He had developed a mediastinal abscess around his heart. Anything he took by mouth leaked into the lining around his lungs, into his chest, and around his heart. They cleaned up the infection as best they could and re-sutured the esophagus to the stomach.

However, no suture line could hold tissue that had been massively infected. Once Michael was in ICU, I could only see him for five minutes. The nurse on duty refused to let me sit in a chair at his bedside just to be with him.

The nurse said I could wait out the night in the waiting room, but without a blanket, pillow, or even a cup of coffee, I decided to go home and return for visiting hours.

Early the next morning, the hospital called to say Michael was in septic shock. The massive infection had spread into his bloodstream and throughout his system. They didn't expect him to live. I asked if they would let me into the ICU as it wasn't visiting hours, and they said yes.

Frantic and distraught, I couldn't find my clothes or my shoes. I prayed fervently that God would not let Michael die before I got there. My mind kept asking how could this be? What happened? What went wrong?

As I walked into his ICU room, Michael was connected to every possible machine, tubes everywhere, monitors, IVs, suction – and of course, the rhythmic noise of the respirator. He looked peaceful. His color was beautiful, and the monitors showed his blood pressure, respirations, and pulse were perfect. Machines controlled his entire being.

As I sat at his bedside and looked around, I reflected on Madeleine Leininger, and Jean Watson, two of my favorite nursing theorists. It is strange the thoughts that come into your head when you are in the middle of a crisis. I wondered what Leininger and Watson would think about the scene taking place if they could see it.

His nurse that day certainly had her work cut out for her. She was attentive to his every need in his unconscious state. However, she did not acknowledge me in any way. She moved around the room as if she were the only one there. Leininger and Watson believe the essence of nursing is caring, that caring is curing, and that the family must be included. Yet not one kind word, not one gentle touch on my shoulder to acknowledge my pain as I sat in the chair beside his bed, holding his hand, and silently weeping.

It wasn't supposed to be like this, he was supposed to be home, recovering, going back to work in a month. Not dying.

Michael survived for ten months, and I often wonder why. Those were months from hell for him and all of us. He endured all the suffering. Completely helpless to do anything for him, we endured watching him suffer.

As a nurse for many years, I had seen much suffering, but never like this. Michael was in and out of the hospital continuously with one complication after another due to the surgery. Whatever they tried to cure caused another problem.

When he wasn't in the hospital, he was at home, and I cared for him. My home looked like an ICU. My kitchen was full of bags of IV fluids, and fluids for tube feedings. I had IV pumps, suction pumps, tube feeding pumps, and boxes of medications to add to his IVs, in addition to what was already added by the pharmacist. I did wound dressing changes for the jpeg tube into his intestine for feedings. He had a porta catheter in his chest for administering IV antibiotics and morphine. Michael could not have anything by mouth for weeks, not even ice chips.

In retrospect, I don't know how I worked full-time as a professor and cared for him as well. I was overwhelmingly frustrated with the doctors, nurses, and healthcare system due to his poor care both at home by the visiting nurse, wound care nurse, and hospital nurses on every unit – except oncology.

Nurses who could not critically think and report concerning findings to the surgeon necessitated Michael being rushed back into ICU due to another episode of sepsis. This was the hospital in which I spent my entire career. I knew the organizational culture, the system, and the politics, yet I could not navigate it. How did others manage who did not have the knowledge I had? Or those who can't speak the language?

Michael developed chronic sepsis from the PICC lines that were used to deliver the tube feedings. He developed sepsis from the porta catheter needed for the delivery of medications. He was in and out of the operating room several times. Another endoscopy revealed the cancer had returned. How was this possible?

In August, Michael's condition was a horror of continuous pain and vomiting and there was nothing I could do for him. The doctor wanted me to keep Michael at home because he thought Michael would pass that night at home. But I couldn't stand to see him suffer, so I called an ambulance. He was admitted to the oncology unit.

To address his pain, a continuous IV with morphine was started. It took twelve hours to get the pain and vomiting under control. He was unconscious most of the time. He wanted to live until his 77th birthday.

Unbelievably, neither the doctors, the surgeon, nor the oncologists told Michael there was nothing more they could do. No one would admit Michael was dying because they made a mistake.

The day before Michael died, I heard the surgeon's voice in the hallway. I was so distressed over the constant battle with the oncologists that I ran out of the door and threw myself into the arms of the surgeon.

"He's dying. They know it. You know it, doctor." I wept hysterically. "But they refused to stop the invasive treatments. The IVs, antibiotics, and pain meds are fine, but please, no more PICC lines, no more port-a-caths. Please, I beg you, let him go."

Knowing a surgical mistake had been made, the medical team felt they had to do every possible treatment to protect themselves from litigation. The surgeon agreed and said he would talk to the oncologists.

Yet, the oncologist had refused to order hospice for us at home, saying, "He is not that bad."

"You had better come over to my home to see what is happening here," I argued.

I had never been so disillusioned with doctors, nurses, and the healthcare system, and in a hospital where I spent my entire career.

The oncology nurses restored my faith in nursing. They were angels of mercy, caring for Michael and me as well, making sure I had something to eat, and encouraging me to take a break and go outside for fresh air. They brought me a chair bed so I could be more comfortable next to my husband.

On Michael's final day, the children had been there earlier to see him. Michael and I had one last conversation. I told him, "There is nothing more the doctors can do for you."

"I knew I was dying when you wouldn't leave my side," he said. "I hoped they could find a cure so I could live."

I shared some regrets.

He told me he wouldn't worry about me as I had the girls, and my grandson, my work, and my horse. "I know you will be okay."

After our talk, he closed his eyes.

I fell asleep in the chair next to him. I awoke suddenly to the sound of Michael struggling to breathe. Though weak, he was determined to get out of bed. I began crying hysterically, trying to prevent him from getting up.

The nurse appeared. "Stop crying," she said. "If he sees you like this, he will not want to leave you."

Quickly, I went to the bathroom, washed my face, dried my eyes, and composed myself.

The nurse suctioned him, administered a sedative, and got him settled. She explained that my distress would prevent him from letting go. I needed to have a calm presence so he would know I would be fine.

For the next several hours, Michael continuously called, "My God, oh my God!"

Distraught, I reached into the drawer for the Bible and flipped pages, looking for favorite passages. None seemed what I needed until I came to Psalm 23. I read that passage continuously.

Ten horrendous months after his first surgery, and two days after his birthday, Michael died.

Psalm 23 comforted and gave me strength to be present through Michael's dying and ultimate death.

"Even though I walk through the darkest valley, I will fear no evil, for you are with me; ..." I did feel death in the room that night – a shadowy presence – it was a battle of life and death, between Lucifer and God, a battle between good and evil, and a fight for Michael's soul. I felt the cold presence of death. I believe God won the battle that night, and Michael went to his heavenly home to be with God.

"In my Father's house are many mansions: if it were not so, I would have told you. I go to prepare a place for you. And if I go and prepare a place for you, I will come again, and receive you unto myself; that where I am, there you may be also," (John 14:1–3).

I was just starting the dissertation phase of my Ph.D. when Michael died. Finishing my dissertation was something he had wanted me to do. It kept me focused on what I had to do, and I believe saved my life.

After I defended my dissertation and received my PhD, I spiraled downward. The work that kept me occupied had ended. I felt lost. Coming home from a favorite Italian restaurant, the thought of living without Michael was more than I could do. I wanted to die. Passing through the highway underpass, I felt a powerful urge to crash my car into the cement embankment.

What good would that do to kill myself?

Michael was gone, and I was left. He was restored to God and at peace. I promised to be with Michael until the end, making sure he did not suffer further. I was with him when he died, but he had to walk the journey himself.

It took five years for the issues surrounding and causing his death to subside. I wanted to sue the hospital for malpractice. Yes, he had cancer, but surgical error was what killed him.

I met with nurse administrators about his abysmal care, I wrote letters to the Hospital Board of Trustees. I reported the surgeon to the state Medical Society; I reported the hospital and surgeon to the Joint Commission. I wrote an article about my experience that was published in a nursing journal. I felt betrayed by the health care system of which I am a part. They were callous, careless, disrespectful, and incompetent.

Infuriated by Michael's ordeal, I met with lawyers. Threatened by my advocacy, the hospital threatened me and my university employer. My university chair advised me to obtain a lawyer after someone from the hospital called and slandered me.

The last lawyer recognized that the hospital felt threatened. He advised that a lawsuit would be extremely difficult. The hospital would claim I was at fault for refusing further treatments. The court would view the surgeon as the expert. It would be difficult to find another expert surgeon to testify against him. There was no guarantee we would win. Assuming the case was valid, settlement could take years.

"You will live with this ongoing case for five or more years," he said. "You will not be able to grieve and find closure."

I dropped the pursuit of justice for Michael to regain my sanity and find closure. At best, winning a wrongful death suit would provide a monetary gain. But what I wanted more than anything was Michael.

My youngest daughter said, "Mother, you did everything you could to fight for Daddy, and he knows that."

I dropped all charges and called the surgeon to tell him. I recognized that the surgeon did not intend to harm. As a trailblazer in his field, his expertise had been beneficial to numerous patients. I forgave him so I could move on.

The autopsy revealed there was no sign of cancer. How could this be? Were they wrong about the diagnosis? A needless death. I never received the answers to what happened that I so desperately needed. I had to find closure without answers and without justice for Michael.

Shortly after his death, on a Saturday afternoon, I was upstairs with the dog by my side. I heard the kitchen door open, and footsteps. I heard the keys to the house placed on the table followed by footsteps again. I thought my grandson had come in.

I called out, but there was no answer. The dog never barked, but jumped off the bed and ran downstairs. I felt afraid, but then I knew it was Michael. Downstairs, the dog stood expectantly at the door. I believe he sensed Michael's spirit.

Alone, I had to take charge of the funeral arrangements. Because Michael had done so much for me, it took more than a year to understand how much money was needed to run the home, buy groceries, take care of the car, taxes, landscaping, and repairs. I laid down with Michael's bathrobe next to me, seeking comfort from this chaotic world I found myself in.

When I think of the stages of grief, isolation is where I struggled the most. When I expressed to my friends or family that Michael was dying, they would say "Don't say that. He's not dying." Was there something wrong with me?

I had never lived by myself. This was hard. Thankfully, I had my beloved dog to keep me company.

I experienced anger toward the surgeons and nurses for the poor care he received. It broke my heart that Michael suffered needlessly. I had episodes of depression. What was I supposed to do without Michael? My life would never be the same.

I felt rejected, excluded, and abandoned by Michael's family, as if I didn't exist to them anymore.

My youngest daughter was my biggest supporter. On days when I became depressed or infuriated because the medical team did not take responsibility, on days when I felt isolated, she was there.

I've experienced grief, depression, acceptance, and anger over and over again. I have been through the acceptance stage of grief and back to depression. I doubt I'll ever be done with grief. Despite the years Michael has been gone, the pain never goes away. The acute physical heartache that I felt for a very long time, has subsided. The lingering poignancy remains, sadness for what once was but is now lost, and will never be again.

I thought having people reach out would be helpful during my grief, but their condolences were not what I needed to feel better about my situation. Though they often asked if there was anything that I needed, the things I needed they couldn't provide.

After the wake, funeral, and burial, I felt friends and family expected me to move on as if nothing happened. Shortly after Michael's death, while I was teaching my Transcultural Nursing course, one of my students insisted on walking me to my car. Class ended at 10:30

p.m., it was dark, and the parking lot close to our building was not busy.

She said her husband waited for her. "We Jewish take care of our widows." Touched by her caring, I will never forget that gesture.

I needed my husband, needed my life back, and needed not to feel the way I felt. This was not something anyone could help resolve.

For years, I talked about Michael to my friends and family. A few years later, I lost my only grandchild. Two major losses in a few years changed the family dynamics tremendously. I lost my mother and my father too. Such huge losses in a decade.

I felt so alone. When I thought I could turn to my friends to fill my needs, they were not there for me. I had two failed relationships after Michael died. Neither man was right for me. I regret wasting time in relationships that were not good for me. I believe I was in such a vulnerable place that I wasn't thinking clearly. To ease the deep loneliness, I sacrificed my sense of self. Those two relationship mistakes were learning experiences, something I needed to learn about life, myself, and relationships. Vulnerable, I couldn't make rational decisions about anything or anybody.

I believe men grieve differently than women. They seem to move on rather quickly. Men need women to take care of their needs. Seldom do you find a widower alone for a long period. Women are self-sufficient. They don't need a man, but it is nice to have a companion. If our man is not available, there is always a female friend.

Content with my life now, I have my girls, my work, my beautiful horse, and my loving dog. My horse was fighting for his life as a newborn when Michael was fighting for his life. When I went to see two-year-old Indy in the field, to see if I liked him, he came right to me. As he looked at me with those large eyes that are pools that go to infinity, I felt Michael coming through. From that moment, Indy and I have been partners. Being at the farm with this noble and majestic creature, I feel in touch with God.

My youngest daughter was instrumental in assisting me to accept my new normal. With a thriving career, she carves time for me. We changed Thanksgiving and holiday traditions since there are only three of us now. We make an annual trip to the Christmas shop in Vermont. We meet for lunch and dinner, and she brings carrots for Indy. My older daughter lives out of state, and I see her, but infrequently. We chat on the phone to keep in touch.

I would tell a new widow to keep busy. The mind needs to be active. If you don't have a full-time job, or desire to have one, get a part-time job, hobby, or enroll in a Bible Study Course.

If you plan to keep your home, do some updates. I repaired sidewalks that Michael had planned to do and hired a landscaper to do what Michael always handled outdoors.

Inside, I changed the kitchen table and chairs. I couldn't look at or sit in Michael's chair. I changed the family room and bought a new bar, added a wide-screen TV, and put a TV in the spare bedroom. Later, I added an electric fireplace to the sitting room. I replaced our bedroom set.

Counseling is a must for the widow, however great, small, short, or long. I found it helpful to talk to someone objective. After my husband died, I cried because of the way he suffered. I cried because no one could take his place and because my life was changed forever.

I felt guilty for not insisting on a second opinion. And guilty for working all those long hours away from him that nurses are required to do. There was guilt for spending so much time going to school, seeking a better quality of life for myself, Michael, and my family.

Tragically, when I left bedside nursing after 30 years and entered academia that offered more time together, Michael died one year later. If only I had known, I never would have spent all that time pursuing a PhD.

In retrospect, if I had not been a nurse, I never would have been able to care for and help my parents, my in-laws, and my husband both physically and emotionally. That was my purpose.

Michael's life impacted me for the good. After he died, when things happened to me that were difficult, I did not have his calming presence by my side to encourage or give me advice. This is what I miss most, sharing everything with Michael.

Life without Michael will never be the same again. Every widow must reinvent herself and make a new life. That is the struggle and it takes time.

Chapter Twenty-One

Life of a Successful Marriage: Helen's Story

M y husband and I married when he was 27 and I was 20 years old. He died at age 77, and I was 70 years old.

We grew up about 120 miles apart, in rural environments. We met in Washington, D.C. where we both had careers working for the Federal Government. Our families got along well and often socialized together.

Seven years older, Bruce retired first and took care of home improvements. He socialized with other retired men and always knew the latest neighborhood news.

Like many African Americans, Bruce had a family history of high blood pressure and cancer. He had surgery for colon cancer at age 38, three eye surgeries for glaucoma, and had problems controlling his blood pressure.

In June 2007, Bruce had his first stroke.[MOU1] His last stroke caused him not to be able to talk, swallow, or eat. I called my brother and sister who came to help me talk with the doctors and the hospital officials about his care and medical directives.

On May 3, 2009, Bruce died in hospice. When he died, I was at peace because he had suffered with many health issues. He was in a better place.

My next-door neighbors have been my support, along with my daughters. My oldest daughter lived in the area, and the two of us would visit Bruce in the nursing home and whenever he was rushed to the hospital. My oldest daughter has rented out her townhouse and lives with me.

I've accepted my husband's death. I wrote a letter expressing things that I feel since he is no longer with me:

My dear late husband,

I hope that when you look back on our marriage that you were happy. A couple of your neighborhood friends said you bragged about me and our two daughters.

There were times when we got into heated disagreements and maybe I should have walked away but that was and still is not my true self. Although you were 27 years old, and I was 20, I didn't want to be treated like you were in control.

I regret that I was not there when you died. But I think God protected me. Both of us had been through many years of sickness and stress.

We had a very good marriage that produced two wonderful daughters. I have no regrets and I don't think you had regrets either.

Your widow

This is a letter to myself looking back on my decisions and actions during my husband's declining health:

Dear Helen,

I cannot think of anything I could have done differently. I made decisions based on whatever was best for Bruce as well as for myself.

After his first stroke, I put him in rehab to regain his ability to walk, but he had another stroke and never regained his ability. He had gotten used to the rehab center and we transferred him to the nursing home in the long-term care ward of the same facility.

I knew I was not able to take care of a person who was paralyzed and unable to walk. My husband was an only child and spoiled by his mother and grandmother. He was somewhat demanding at the nursing home, and I would smooth things for him with the staff. I wanted to make sure he remained comfortable and that he received excellent care.

When my husband was in the facility, he told me I was the best wife in the world.

After my husband died the transition was very hard initially. While he was in the nursing home, I visited often. After his death, I spent time with family and friends. I volunteered at my State's Welcome Center's Information Desk and joined the Red Hat Society.

I enjoy living in the same home and neighborhood. I had the walls painted and carpet removed. A longtime friend who loves to decorate staged my house. We moved large pieces of furniture around and purchased small items so the home looked different. Making those changes helped emotionally.

Therapy helped me learn to make decisions, oversee major maintenance repairs on the house that Bruce had always done, and realize I didn't have to do everything. I chose to work with a counselor who was a few years older than me and who had also lost her husband.

I found out that I had to let people have the freedom to say what they wanted to say in their condolence remarks.

My advice to other widows is to be good to yourself and feel good about yourself. What is important to you at this stage of your life? Get busy doing what you enjoy.

I enjoyed talking with people, especially those travelers that came to the Welcome Center.

I have heard that you need to wait a year before making important decisions such as selling your home. For that reason, I think widows should wait a year before getting married because marriage is as important as deciding to sell your home. Give yourself time to grieve and make important decisions.

Also, your adult children and in-laws are in deep grief. You may appear to them as if you did not love your child's parent, or the in-laws may think you didn't deeply love their child if you move on quickly.

If you decide to marry again and have small children, choose a man who loves your children and can be a wonderful father to them.

Children are precious gifts from God. Always be protective of their emotional happiness and welfare so they grow to be happy, content, well-adjusted, productive, and successful young men and women. Have a prenuptial agreement, or a will so your children receive their father's inheritance.

If you have dreams and career goals, consider staying single. Many men lack the courage to love a strong, successful woman. Additionally, men tend to expect certain actions from a wife. Having the time to concentrate on the career may mean remaining single.

Chapter Twenty-Two

A Remarkable Journey: Catherine's Story

C ancer. Hearing the diagnosis from the oncologist was a shock. Immediately, I remembered the promise God gave me two years prior from a passage in the book of Luke. "I have come to heal him." I shared that revelation with my husband, and it comforted him with hope and expectancy.

Each week, my husband reported to the hospital with me by his side to have radiation to his upper chest. At the eighth session, he began to smell burning, a cooking smell. After ten weeks of radiation, he had visible burns on his back and his lungs were filling with fluid which required draining procedures.

Ten sessions of radiation took a toll and he was in and out of the hospital for three weeks.

One particular night he struggled for air. I prayed, asking God to help him breathe. Seeing him suffer was difficult. The Holy Spirit said it was time to release my husband because of the pain he endured.

Though I did not want to do this, I did. Our final conversation was beautiful.

"I hear your struggle through the night, and I don't want to see you suffer anymore." I assured him that if he had to go it was okay. The children and I would be okay and I would see him on the other side.

Alex smiled. "I know that's right."

We loved each other so much, and having to let go was something we never saw coming. The doctor brought hospice in to talk to me. I filled out a lot of paperwork.

Within four hours, many of our friends and family came. They sang which seemed to comfort him. The two girls and I stayed behind after the others left. When my husband knew he was having an episode he lovingly motioned the girls to leave the room because he did not want them to see what he knew was inevitable.

My husband only had two sessions of chemo before he died. Today, if anything ever happened to me on that level, I would refuse radiation because of what it did to my husband.

Six months after his diagnosis, on June 30th, 2009, he took his last breath in my arms. While we talked, he laid his head on my breast. With a look up to heaven and a soft sigh, he was gone. Losing him was so hard but his transition was gracefully beautiful and peaceful.

"Who would have ever thought you would see the face of Jesus before me?" I went into shock at that moment, and the Holy Spirit covered me with a special grace.

I didn't cry when he died. After the numbness wore off, I cried deeper than I had ever cried in my life. I didn't know anyone could have that many tears. It was as if I was dead yet functioning. Scrip-

121

tures were a blur and I could not understand why my eyes would not function to read the Bible. All I seemed able to do was journal throughout the day and listen to the audio Bible every night.

As I journaled, I was able to be authentic and raw with my feelings. The Holy Spirit would finish what I started writing. This was a comfort, knowing God felt my pain and carried me. Journaling became my counselor for my grief.

I struggled with faith after God did not heal Alex. I thought I was going to die after my mother and grandmother died, but I got through it. Would my faith get me through the death of Alex?

"God," I cried, "I feel like I can't breathe. Save me."

A friend invited me to California three months after Alex died. When I returned home it hit me that Alex was not there to pick me up from the airport. The reality further hit home when I put the key in the front door, and he was not there to greet me. My heart was not connected to my reality.

After four months I went back to work at my church. I was still in a grief-stricken place. I needed more time. Normality hurts. I decided to go to my aunt's church for a couple of months. Going to my own church held too many memories of what once was. When I did return, I sat with my mother-in-law at the back of the church.

A guest preacher spoke. He said, "I want all the married people to stand."

That didn't include me anymore.

Next, he said, "I want all the single people to stand."

Was I a single person? I did not know who I was. After the service I cried all the way home. "Lord," I asked, "Who am I?"

"You are a widow," came His reply. "Remember what I said? I have something special for you."

I searched Scriptures pertaining to widows. This was comforting because I found I belonged to a group. I had to embrace that place.

After my husband's death, my whole life as I knew seemed erased. I had no goals or dreams. My faith shattered. Yet, God helped me.

During the grieving and healing process, I had many dialogues with God. I questioned Him about things I believed He said to me. Prior to my husband's death, I heard God say, "In just a little while I'm going to do something for you that I promised." I thought a miracle was going to take place and Alex would be healed.

"I did answer your prayers," I felt God say. "I came and healed Alex. He'll never be sick again. Alex is with me, and I am still with you."

I will be forever appreciative of the help I received from a hospice grief counselor as well as group counseling.

A lifeline during my grief, people telephoned, visited, and took me for a movie or a meal. Even going to a hair appointment was a change of environment. When grief sapped my strength, family and friends took care of chores around the house and made life bearable.

I found it helpful each time someone said, "Catherine, I'm sorry for your loss." Sometimes people looked at me and said absolutely nothing while their hearts spoke unspeakable empathy. Wordless hugs were deeply felt. Their care and concern for me came through.

One coworker hugged me so compassionately, I knew it was God using him to comfort me. Another friend sat silently with me. God sent everything I needed without me realizing I needed it. God gave me what I could not ask for.

Some let me know they were there for me but confessed that they did not know my pain. They listened without overly spiritualizing everything, which allowed me time to grieve without judgment. They often sat with me quietly, waiting patiently for whatever I needed.

I received numerous cards and letters sent to console me and my family. I couldn't read them at the time, but while I was grieving, I received their written love and sincerity.

I slept with my Bible close to my heart even though I could not read it. God promised to heal broken hearts. I journaled what I felt and cried while praying and having conversations with God. Reading the Bible and books on grief helped me understand that what I was feeling and experiencing was normal.

Many people told me their memories of Alex. As if hungry to be fed more memories, I sat for hours. I loved him even more when I heard their stories about him.

After they left, I put on a piece of Alex's clothing. I could smell him, which brought a nearness even though he was gone. I kissed a photo of him every night to keep alive the promise we made to each other. I slept with a pillow my daughter made with our picture on it.

Listening to others grieve brought back a flood of memories. Nonetheless, I would listen to those who lost a spouse as they shared their stories. Although I did not interject my experiences with Alex's death at the time, I recalled each trial and tear they shed as they spoke from a place of brokenness that I knew well.

When I returned to work, I felt fearful to take the metro. No matter where Alex worked, he had always taken me to and from work. Eventually, I found new friends on the train. Though work was stressful, I needed a new normal. Getting into a new pattern benefited me greatly from smelling flowers to cleaning the house, walking, and going to the grocery store.

I had to learn to do things without Alex. Hanging out with my good friends, and taking vacations were things I did to implement my new normal. When I encouraged others and prayed aloud for someone, it helped me. I started reading my Bible more deeply and getting revelation again. This enabled me to believe God without the fear of losing someone else I loved. I found comfort in attending church among a crowd of people that knew my husband had died.

Spending time with my family, serving others, ministry, and teaching on topics other than grief and loss, getting up early in the morning to meet with God, prayer, journaling, and walking became my new life.

In my anguish over a prayer request that God did not honor the way I would have liked, I trusted that He knew what was best. This allowed me to continue my faith journey.

Once in a dark place, it was bitterly cold and I felt numb. God allowed the air to brush my cheekbones, just enough to let me know I was alive and not alone. He is in the air I breathe, even when the wind is cold. God told me that He covers me. Even in the dark places, as I read my Bible, God gives revelation about Him and about myself.

I've learned to accept that Alex is dead and to deal with all the pain. This is a letter I wrote to my deceased husband Alex:

Dear Alex,

Losing you was the hardest thing I ever had to endure. Words cannot describe the pain, emptiness, and fear I had to endure being without you. The best way that I can explain this experience is to say I know hell is real. Why? Because it felt like I tasted some of it after you died.

The suffering and watching the children and grands grieve over you was another blow to my already broken and shattered heart. I can truly say that during the season of my grief, I began to understand even more the significance of why Christ came to earth. Why He died and rose again. So that He could one day stop death forever.

Although we did not get the chance to talk about what we would do if one of us died, I know without a doubt that your desire was for us to continue to enjoy life as we did while together.

Alex, until that day we meet together in glory, memories of you will always be in my heart.

Love, Catherine

In the program for his going-home celebration, I wrote, "To my husband, companion, friend, lover, provider, and protector. I will always love you." These few words could never reveal the depth of my respect, love, and honor I have for "my sweetie," as I often called him. A wonderful husband and father, for 30 years he did everything with thought and care for the children and me, supporting us with enthusiasm, excitement, and love. The depth of our love for one another will forever be a gift from God.

Looking back, there is nothing that I can think of that I would have done differently, even when I did not agree with Alex when he wanted to invest money in an old beat-up apartment building. As I'm recalling this I laugh out loud.

I did everything that God helped and taught me to do for my husband. In our early years of marriage, there were times that if it were up to me, I would have walked away. The Lord knows I am so glad that I decided to do it God's way and trust him to make our marriage incredible and remarkable.

My advice for a widow is to be gentle with yourself. Do not force what you used to do. Don't think it's strange that you don't feel that way anymore. Let God walk you through this new path and let God carry you to different places.

Do things that make you feel better. God is a lifter of your head and a deliverer of your broken heart. Be obedient to whatever He tells you to do.

Let go of misery. If you don't, misery will destroy you.

Don't be afraid to allow something new in your life.

Give yourself permission to be happy. Watch movies that make you laugh. Read books about loss that help you understand what you're feeling. Help someone else.

Find something about your late husband that makes you smile when you think about him. The songs *I Hope You Dance* and *Tell Your Heart to Beat Again* remind me of Alex and what he would want for me, and that makes me smile.

Move forward in life. Sometimes moving forward means letting go of the past. Consider changing things to nake the house look different than when you and your husband lived there together.

A year after Alex died, I heard God tell me to move furniture around and get rid of old things. One day the hook broke in the master closet and the clothes dropped to the floor. Alex's clothes were still in the closet and God orchestrated the reason I needed to pass his things on. I was able to make room to move forward. Letting go doesn't mean I forgot him, but made room to add in new things.

Don't pick up old bad habits. I picked up a habit of secluding myself and eating dinner in my room. I no longer had anyone to cook for and as a result, I gained 15 pounds.

Finally, be willing to trust God. Alex died five years before my retirement. I was very fearful of how I was going to make it. The Lord said, "Do you trust me? It really wasn't your income that sustained you in the first place, and it wasn't your husband's income that sustained you. It was me." I stepped out on faith and retired.

I had heard my pastor say one time that you can't beat God giving no matter how hard you try. So, I kept giving for a whole five years from both salaries and God blessed me beyond measure. I kept giving tithes. I had no financial pressures. My provision came from God's hands to my hands.

Trust God. I know you are hurting, but trust that He loves you more than you'll ever know. Nothing is too hard for Him. He's a promise keeper who says in Psalm 30:11, "You turned my wailing into dancing; you removed my sackcloth and clothed me with joy."

I hope you dance.

Chapter Twenty-Three

The Peace of God: Irene's Story

My husband and I met at my aunt and uncle's gas station and used car lot where I worked.

Having recently finished serving in the Army, he drove in, looking for a car. He bought a car and got my phone number. In his version of the story, he described that on that fateful afternoon, I washed his windshield and it was love at first sight.

We dated for four years, married, and our first daughter was born a year later. During the 47 years of our wonderful marriage, we were blessed with two additional daughters. A relationship with Jesus and being active in our church were important to both of us.

One Saturday morning, Derek was in an accident. A few days later, he passed away.

Through faith, I was blessed with wisdom, guidance, and comfort to get through this incomprehensible phase of life. "God is our refuge and strength, an ever-present help in trouble, Psalm 46:1." We all process grief differently, but I hope that sharing what helped me through this difficult time will also help you. Derek and I were people of faith so God's Word and being active at church were personally comforting. Keeping busy has also been crucial to my healing.

Reading the Bible every day, especially in the morning, helps me to focus on the Lord and gives me peace and strength for the day. I highly recommend joining a Bible study, whether you are new to faith or a mature believer in Jesus Christ.

These are verses I cling to:

"It is good to praise the Lord
and make music to your name, O Most High,
[2] proclaiming your love in the morning
and your faithfulness at night,
[3] to the music of the ten-stringed lyre
and the melody of the harp.
[4] For you make me glad by your deeds, Lord;
I sing for joy at what your hands have done.
[5] How great are your works, Lord,
how profound your thoughts!
[6] Senseless people do not know,
fools do not understand,
[7] that though the wicked spring up like grass
and all evildoers flourish,
they will be destroyed forever.
[8] But you, Lord, are forever exalted.
[9] For surely your enemies, Lord,
surely your enemies will perish;

all evildoers will be scattered.

10 You have exalted my horn[b] like that of a wild ox;

fine oils have been poured on me.

11 My eyes have seen the defeat of my adversaries;

my ears have heard the rout of my wicked foes.

12 The righteous will flourish like a palm tree,

they will grow like a cedar of Lebanon;

13 planted in the house of the Lord,

they will flourish in the courts of our God.

14 They will still bear fruit in old age,

they will stay fresh and green,

15 proclaiming, "The Lord is upright;

he is my Rock, and there is no wickedness in him," Psalm 92:1-15.

"Be strong and courageous. Do not be afraid or terrified because of them, for the Lord your God goes with you; he will never leave you nor forsake you," Deuteronomy 31: 6.

"There is a time for everything,

and a season for every activity under the heavens:

2   a time to be born and a time to die,

a time to plant and a time to uproot,

3   a time to kill and a time to heal,

a time to tear down and a time to build,

4   a time to weep and a time to laugh,

a time to mourn and a time to dance,

⁵   a time to scatter stones and a time to gather them,

a time to embrace and a time to refrain from embracing," Ecclesiastes 3:1-5.

" I can do all this through him who gives me strength," Philippians 4:13.

" Peace I leave with you; my peace I give you. I do not give to you as the world gives. Do not let your hearts be troubled and do not be afraid," John 14:27.

"Those who sow with tears

will reap with songs of joy.

⁶ Those who go out weeping,

carrying seed to sow,

will return with songs of joy,

carrying sheaves with them," Psalm 126:5-6

"For I know the plans I have for you," declares the Lord, "plans to prosper you and not to harm you, plans to give you hope and a future," Jeremiah 29:11

"And the God of all grace, who called you to his eternal glory in Christ, after you have suffered a little while, will himself restore you and make you strong, firm and steadfast," 1 Peter 5:10

"Finally, brothers and sisters, rejoice! Strive for full restoration, encourage one another, be of one mind, live in peace. And the God of love and peace will be with you," 2 Corinthians 13:11.

My advice to widows is to get involved. At my church, I joined the weekly widow's group. These ladies were welcoming, offered comfort, and were the hands and feet of Jesus in my life. I rarely miss a week and treasure the bond I share with them.

I also attended the church senior group, 55 Alive. Beyond the great trips, delicious food, fun, and fellowship we enjoyed, these friendships are among the most special in my life. I also served on the hospitality team, assisting with weekly meals and helping with special events.

If you don't have a church family, this might be the perfect time to look for one. Ask a friend or neighbor if you can attend a service with them.

Don't wait for someone to ask you to dinner or a movie, reach out and invite them. I frequently ask my friends to do fun activities.

Be busy by being a blessing. When I served others, I was too preoc-
cupied with the task to think about ourselves and the effects of losing
a husband. I watch two of my granddaughters several days each week.

Do you have friends or family members who could use your help?
Is there someone who would appreciate a meal you made for them?

Look in your community for volunteer opportunities such as
Meals on Wheels, reading to children or seniors at your local library
or senior, or serving at a local food bank. There is no shortage of
volunteer work in any community. You can make a difference.

I pray that you will find hope and comfort in the Lord during this
time of sadness and loss.

Chapter Twenty-Four

Prayer of Faith

I would be remiss if I did not pray for those of you who are reading this book who do not know Jesus Christ as your personal Lord and Savior. You may not know what it is to know Him as the God of all comfort.

It is necessary to have a personal relationship with Him to receive all the rights and benefits of being his daughter.

Father, I call upon You in this hour, to use me to speak words of life and light to any woman who is not a believer, is not saved, or simply put, has not asked Jesus to forgive her sins, come into her heart, and dwell with her. I know that it is your will that none should perish and that all should come to the saving knowledge of Jesus Christ.

Father, I bring her before your throne and ask you to empower her that she would pray this prayer of faith and believe the power that resides in your Word so she will become saved, with all the promises and purposes You have been waiting to bestow upon her.

I call upon Your Word which is alive, to soften her heart so that when she reads these Scriptures and repeats this prayer, they will take up residence with her.

John 3:16-17 "For God so loved the world that he gave his only Son, that whoever believes in him should not perish but have eternal life. For God did not send his Son into the world to condemn the world, but in order that the world might be saved through him."

Romans 6:23 "For the wages of sin is death, but the gift of God is eternal life Christ Jesus our Lord."

Romans 3:23 "For all have sinned and fall short of the glory of God."

Romans 5:8 "But God demonstrates His own love toward us, in that while we were yet sinners, Christ died for us."

Romans 10: 9-10 "If you declare with your mouth, "Jesus is Lord," and believe in your heart that God raised him from the dead, you will be saved. For it is with your heart that you believe and are justified, and it is with your mouth that you profess your faith and are saved."

If your heart has been touched by the prayer that I prayed for you, repeat these words:

"Jesus, I believe that You are the Son of God and Savior of the world. I believe that You died for my sins and that You rose from the dead. I ask You to forgive me of my sins and fill me with Your Holy Spirit. Today I choose to follow you for the rest of my life as Lord and Savior. Amen."

I rejoice with you, sister, in your confession, as all of heaven is now rejoicing.

Chapter Twenty-Five

Guided Prayers

There are times when the words just don't come. Romans 8:26 describes, "the Spirit helps us in our weakness. We do not know what we ought to pray for, but the Spirit himself intercedes for us through wordless groans."

Come to the Lord with your pain, your loss, your tears. Pour out your heart. Sometimes that will be with words. On other occasions the Holy Spirit understands your weeping and groans. For the days guided prayer is beneficial, speak the prayers below to the God above.

Father, thank you for the life I shared with my husband, and for this life after his death. I ask that You give me clarity of mind. Help me treasure the memories of those precious moments when we were together. Strengthen me as I find a new direction for the next chapters of my life.

I pray this in Jesus' name. Amen.

Father, You knew when I would be born and when I would meet my husband. You knew when we would marry and when our life together would end. You provide everything I need to walk the journey without him. You have generously given me the gift of Your presence.

I pray this in Jesus' name. Amen.

Thank You, Lord, for the wisdom You give to me now. You are Jehovah Rapha, the One who heals my heart. My loss is raw and real. I ask that you do for me, "immeasurably more than what they could ask or think, according to his power that is at work within us," Ephesians 3:20.

In Jesus' name. Amen.

Heal me of painful flashbacks. So often when I mention something painful about the past, I hurt all over again as if it just happened yesterday.

Bottle my tears and create a river of blessings that overflow each time I cry. Life will never be the same without my husband, but You have the power to make it better. Your word promises that we can have life more abundantly. You are a promise keeper. Help me walk by faith in difficult days ahead.

In Jesus' name. Amen.

God, like any wound that has been re-injured, I pray You seal up this overwhelming hurt. I feel paralyzed since my husband's death. Help me move forward. Do immeasurably more than I can ask or think in the years to come.

I pray this in the matchless name of Jesus Christ. Amen.

Father, I believe You allowed me to live because my life still has a purpose. Provide comfort. Swallow up this deep sadness and replace it with joy too vast to measure.

Thank You for helping other women who will find themselves alone. Like me, many won't know what to do. Holy Spirit, You brought comfort and direction, showing me which way to go. I pray You guide others and comfort them through the Holy Spirit.

In your Son's name, Jesus Christ. Amen.

Father, thank You for the people You brought into my life by divine appointment. Only You know how connections lead to other connections within Your master plan.

We are women who find ourselves without husbands, and we are women still standing and moving forward so we can help others. I never envisioned empowering women through widowhood. Yet, that's the gift that You've given to me. God, You comfort me so I can comfort others with the comfort I've been given.

In Jesus' name. Amen.

DR. CLARISE HAIRSTON OTTLEY

Thank You for the good moments, bad times, and sad seasons. Thank You for the richness that has come as a result of these experiences.

Thank You for the wisdom and peace You blanketed over me.

In Jesus' name. Amen.

Help me live out my days without spending too much time in the past. As the master and controller of my life, help me live each day in the moment.

I yield to You in this new chapter, looking forward with the expectation of greatness because of the promise You made to me before the world was created.

In Jesus' name. Amen.

Father, as I take this journey I pray for Your full authority over every moment of my past, present, and future. Please manifest Your love for me in a tangible way.

You have an even greater plan for my life than what I have ever experienced. Help me see through Your eyes the new things You are doing (Psalm 43:18-20).

In Jesus' name. Amen.

140

I pray for my faith to be strengthened during this season. Help me trust You every day and every moment. Let me not lean on or yield to my own understanding of what direction I should take. Come Holy Spirit, please lead and guide me. Thank You for the affirmation to walk with expectancy for all the great things You have in store.

In Jesus' name. Amen.

God, thank You for the revelations You give. There is much more ahead for me. Guide me to walk in obedience to the Holy Spirit. You have purpose for me. Guide my every move and decision.

For those moments when I feel lonely, restore the joy that only comes from You. Jehovah Roi, You know me, love me, and see me. I pray for wholeness, and that You meet all my needs according to Your riches in Glory.

In Jesus' name. Amen

Father, You said You know our thoughts before we think them. You said You came to heal the brokenhearted. Seal up the painful memories that surface. Bind my heart with Your healing balm.

In Jesus' name, Amen.

Father, You are the God of all comfort. Nothing is hidden from You. Help me take every thought captive and free my mind so I will not suffer any recoil. Replace thoughts of sadness with thoughts of You.

In Jesus' name. Amen.

You're a good God. You know what I need before I ask. Do what You do best. Heal, deliver, and set me free to share at every opportunity that You are Lord. You reign supreme in every circumstance. I give You glory and praise. There are no situations that are out of Your control. Not even this.

In Jesus' name. Amen.

"Where, O death, is your victory? Where, O death, is your sting?" I Corinthians 15:4.

Thank You, God, for the love You had for my husband and the love You have for me.

"Greater love has no one than this: to lay down one's life for one's friends," says John 15:13. You laid down Your life that no one should perish. In the triumphant years ahead, help me proclaim that You are King of kings and Lord of lords. My life is in Your hands. Give me the strength to carry out Your purpose and will.

In Jesus' name. Amen.

God, let the sting of being reminded of my horrible loss be Your tool to give strength and hope to other widows.

Your Word says in Romans 8:28, "*All* things work together for the good to them that love God, to them who are the called, according to his purpose." It's not good that my husband died, but You will make good come out of his death because of Your love for me.

In Jesus' name. Amen.

For myself and other women who are also widows, I pray for Your blessings to pour out so there are too many to receive. Restore peace beyond what we could ask or think.

In Jesus' name. Amen.

Father in You I put my trust. There is no way I could have made this journey without You. Seal up open wounds that need your healing touch. I pray for emotional protection. Of myself, I am weak, but You Oh Lord are strong. I draw the needed strength to go on without my husband from You. I am thankful for Your grace and mercy.

In Jesus' name I pray. Amen.

"Record my misery; list my tears on your scroll,' are they not in your record?" In Psalm 56:8, You say You catch my tears in a bottle and each tear has meaning to You. Out of the depths of my heart, I have cried. Yet even when the pain was too deep to be expressed, You knew exactly what it meant.

There is no way I can do this without Your strength. You are Jehovah Jireh, my provider. You promised that you would comfort me. I did not understand what level of strength I would need until my husband died. You promised that when I walked through the valley of the shadow of death, You would be right there with me.

Whatever I have to go through without my husband's protection, be my Husband as You promised in Your word. Help me trust that you will meet every need.

In Jesus' name. Amen.

When I recall the pain of my husband's death, it's as if I'm reliving the moments as when they first occurred. Everything about that dreadful day will forever be etched in my mind. I ask You, Father, to remove the sting.

In Jesus' name. Amen.

God, some days the loss of my husband feels like it is still raw. The pain of his death is yet fresh in my mind and the tears come. By Your Holy Spirit, provide comfort as You promised in Psalm 147:3, "He heals the brokenhearted and binds up their wounds."

In Jesus' name. Amen.

Father, I pray for the broken hearts of fellow widows who seek comfort. Losing a spouse to an illness or suddenly is stressful and layered with emotional turmoil.

You, God, know all things. You are omniscient. You are fully aware of our journey without our husbands. As David said in Psalms 139:1-2, "You know me, you've searched me." Guard my heart and mind. Bind thoughts that cause emotional harm.

In Jesus' name. Amen.

God of all comfort, You listen for my every cry. Turn Your ear to me today. You know what my life has been like since my husband died. Strengthen and equip me with Your love and hope so I can move forward.

In Jesus' name. Amen.

Father, You said that You are a father to the fatherless and a husband to the widow. Protect my footsteps wherever you take me. My heart feels broken beyond repair. Yet, you can mend the break, and give fresh purpose. When all hope seems lost, remind me I can trust You with my deepest sorrow. Bring me through this wilderness and to the promised land that You have prepared.

In Jesus' name. Amen.

Father God, pour out Your Holy Spirit to fill the empty places that opened wide when my husband died. Thank You for the countless ways You've carried and sustained me, even when I didn't realize I was being carried. Comfort me through the empty days and lonely nights.

In Jesus' name. Amen.

Father, it is through Your grace and mercy that I can move forward after the death of my husband. Comfort me as only You can do. Open doors that lead to the path You have already prepared for me. Increase my faith and provide a strong foundation to build upon. The saying goes, "When all you have is God, you will discover He is all you need."

Be my Lord, keep my heart and mind in harmony with Yours.

In Jesus' name. Amen.

Chapter Twenty-Six

References

- Depression: NIMH=21-MH-8079, 02/2021

- Dexter, Louie, BA, Karolina Brook, MD and Elizabeth Frates, MD. *The Laughter Prescription*. American Journal Lifestyle Med. 2016. June 23. doi: 10.1177/15698276145 50279

- United States Conference of Catholic Bishops (USCCB) https://bible.usccb.org/bible/deuteronomy/31

Acknowledgements

I would like to thank the women who courageously shared their stories with me and with the world. Ten brave women who, like me, thought of the countless women who would one day find themselves as widows. What could we say that would help to comfort their broken hearts? May the words God laid on our hearts, recorded in this book, be a healing balm as they look to Him for that touch. We are merely God's conduits.

Though this task was far from easy, you did the hard work. You put other widows above your pain of recalling your husband's death. Now they will find strength for the journey that lies ahead of them because of what you shared.

May God heal you again for the heart-wrenching pain that having to recall your husband's death has brought you. This I know, your selfless desire to help widows will assist them to move forward.

About the Author

Dr. Clarise H. Ottley served as Clinical Coordinator and Nursing Director for the Mother/Baby Unit and serves as a Nurse Educator for the Center for Learning and Development at West Virginia University Hospital.

A Professor of Nursing for 12 years at Shepherd University, she worked as Project Director of Grants in the Division of Nursing at Health Resources & Services Administration. She earned her PhD in Nursing Research from Duquesne University.

Clarise is the mother of four amazing sons and six precious grandchildren.

Made in the USA
Middletown, DE
30 August 2024

59652047R00086